WHAT'S LOVE GOT
TO DO WITH IT?

WHAT'S LOVE GOT TO DO WITH IT?

Emotions and Relationships in Popular Songs

Thomas J. Scheff

Paradigm Publishers

Boulder, London

Copyright © 2011 by Paradigm Publishers

Published in the United States by Paradigm Publishers, 2845 Wilderness Place, Boulder, Colorado 80301 USA.

Paradigm Publishers is the trade name of Birkenkamp & Company, LLC, Dean Birkenkamp, President and Publisher.

Library of Congress Cataloging-in-Publication Data

Scheff, Thomas J.
  What's love got to do with it? : emotions and relationships in popular songs / Thomas J. Scheff.
    p. cm.
  Includes bibliographical references and index.
  ISBN 978-1-59451-815-7 (hardcover : alk. paper)
  ISBN 978-1-59451-816-4 (pbk : alk. paper)
  1. Popular music—History and criticism. 2. Love songs—History and criticism. 3. Emotions in music. I. Title.
ML3470.S33 2010
782.42164'159—dc22

                                                                    2010019006

Printed and bound in the United States of America on acid-free paper that meets the standards of the American National Standard for Permanence of Paper for Printed Library Materials.

Designed and Typeset by Straight Creek Bookmakers.

14 13 12 11   5 4 3 2

CONTENTS

Preface: A Note to the Reader   *vii*

Acknowledgments   *xiii*

1   Introduction: What's in a Love Song?   1

2   Conceptions of Love: The Eternal Debate   17

3   Emotion Languages: Love, Pride, Anger, Grief,
    Fear, and Other Emotions   43

4   Alienation in Top 40 Songs 1930–2000   59

5   Nobody Knows but Me: Curtailment of Feeling   93

6   Genuine Love and Connectedness   103

7   What Emotion Is the Shadow of Love?   121

8   The Beat Goes On: Alienation and Curtailment
    of Emotions   131

Afterword: Two Projects for Better Lyrics   147

References   151

Index   157

About the Author   166

PREFACE

A Note to the Reader

This book seeks to increase our understanding of popular songs and their effects on those who listen to them. In years of teaching college students, I couldn't help but notice that for many of them, these popular songs held a special meaning, as they did to me when I was their age. Here is a comment by a twenty-year-old:

> I grew up listening to *NSYNC, Backstreet Boys, Spice Girls and Britney Spears. Their songs defined my life. My friends and I would know every single word, beat, and dance move. We would religiously sit in front of the TV and wait to see if our favorite song had made it to Number 1. In high school, my friends and I were fascinated with the popular bands. We bought CDs, merchandise, concerts, and TV show appearances. Listening to the songs on repeat and knowing every word became our afterschool passion. (Lauren Tokushige)

Over the years, I heard many similar testimonies, that popular songs were much more meaningful to them than most of the other arenas of their lives. In my own case when I was their age, and for many of my students, these songs had an intense private meaning that would have been difficult to put into words. It occurred to me that I might learn a great deal if I studied the most popular of the popular songs, the Top 40, and the meaning they held for my students and their larger audience. Perhaps I could learn something important about myself, the students, and the society that we live in.

My idea was that collecting and discussing popular song lyrics with students might be a way not only of understanding the lyrics, but also of providing entry into the lives of the students, and in that way, into the workings of our society. I found that my primary interest was less in understanding the lyrics themselves and more in the students, their understanding of the songs and what meaning the songs had for them. It soon proved to be the case that discussing song lyrics was a direct path into the students' lives, not just their outer lives, their workplace, friendships, family, and romantic relationships, but also their inner lives.

The first aim of this book is to use popular lyrics as a mirror, perhaps a magnifying glass, that will shed light on the nature of our society. The second aim is explore ways in which our society might be changed by helping students understand themselves and others better, and by encouraging the invention of new kinds of popular lyrics and other forms of art and media. Although this book has little to say about film and still less about TV, the underlying principles may well be the same.

What makes popular songs popular? In most cases, artistic and educational values don't seem to matter. My background in the sociology of emotions suggested to me that what matters is *emotions*, on the one hand, and *relationships*, on the other. Lyrics that evoke unresolved feelings of love, pride, grief, anger, and other emotions have dominated the popular charts for many years.

More subtly, these lyrics also involve the *relationship* with the loved one, implying closeness. Surprisingly, however, upon inspection many of the relationships implied can be seen as not close. In fact, it will be clear that the relationships implied in most love lyrics are alienated, but the lack of closeness is disguised and hidden.

Drawing these two components together, popular love lyrics present a picture of an imagined *social-emotional world*. The nature of basic emotions and relationships will be outlined at some length, since they are little understood in modern societies. My many years of study of the social-emotional world have suggested that modern societies tend to ignore this world. Thought, perception, behavior, and the material world come first, emotions and relationships, last.

Similarly, since modern societies are highly individualistic, the nature of relationships usually takes a backseat to qualities of individuals. Unlike traditional societies, where the focus is on social relationships, modern societies focus on the self-reliant individual. The usual treatment of the social-emotional world in modern societies is limited, casual, and I have found, often misleading.

A 2000 cartoon in the *New Yorker* magazine portrays this situation graphically. A man lying on a psychoanalyst's couch is saying: "Look, call it denial if you like, but I think what goes on in my personal life is none of my own damn business." In modern societies, behavior, thought, and the material world are our business, but not emotions and relationships.

This book compares the imagined emotional world of popular songs with a more realistic world of emotions and relationships that I have glimpsed as a social scientist, and offers suggestions toward improving both worlds.

You will note that many of the lyric quotes in this book are quite brief, usually only two lines. This kind of abbreviation seemed necessary because of copyright restrictions. Two lines, but no more, are deemed "Fair Use" without copyright permission. I was willing to do this because the complete lyrics are readily available at no cost to the reader on one or another of the many, many online lyric Web sites. If you want to see a complete lyric, just Google the title. In most cases, you will find not only the words, but also the music.

Which brings up one of the limitations of my approach. Although occasionally there will be a mention of the relation between the words and music of a particular song, this book is overwhelmingly about words, not music. I am not a musician myself, so I have been unable to provide a sustained analysis of an important part of the popular song world.

In my experience teaching classes on this world, the students are at first taken aback, because they are more involved with the music, especially the beat. So early in the class we listen to the music. Since the sixties, the music has become more and more dominant over the words. However, after only a few discussions of the lyrics, most of the students become captivated in the quest to understand the words, and at least in class, more or less forget about the music, as I have in this book. A second limitation involves the type of song that is in focus. This book concerns the meaning of popular song lyrics, particularly the genre known as pop: the most popular of the popular songs, as determined by the Top 40 ratings. Most of the examples come from the yearly Top 40 lists, but there are also examples from the less popular songs. Although two other genres are mentioned, rap and hip-hop, little attention is given to genres, such as country and western. The book focuses on pop because its lyrics are known by the greatest number of people, and therefore it should best inform us on the nature of the society in which we live.

A Note to Teachers of Social Science
and Their Students

Although this book is written for all readers, young and old, some high school or college students may read it as part of their classroom assignments. Other readers may wish to skip ahead now to Chapter 1. Students and teachers may want to consider what follows. I continue here with remarks on how a social science perspective can be applied to better understand our lives.

This book is designed so that it can be used in a course that introduces social science to high school and college students. The topic is one that will attract student interest, since many students are already experts on popular songs, and may also be deeply emotionally involved with them. The treatment here, however, will be news to practically all of them. The next few pages of this preface will outline this treatment so readers will know what to expect.

Two main social science points will be made in the treatment. The first concerns the strengths and weaknesses of ordinary language. One of the reasons that popular songs are popular is that they use ordinary, rather than technical, language. But every living language is a fountainhead of both wisdom and error, and modern English is no exception. Although it contains by far the largest number of words than any other language, it turns out that English has fewer emotion words than many smaller languages, and the emotion words it contains are often at least ambiguous and at times confusing and obfuscating.

A social science treatment of emotions offers terms that are more clearly defined. Emotions described in this way, using technical terms rather than the usual words, will seem a bit unwieldy at first. But with a little practice, one can see many advantages, such as not confusing one emotion with another, and in noticing, naming, and discussing emotions that are ordinarily not visible enough to be discussed.

The second point of the social science treatment concerns the individualism that is taken for granted in modern societies. Like the English-speaking society in which the Top 40 songs are sung, they focus on the self-contained individual, ignoring, for the most part, the web of social relationships in which every individual is involved. The nature of the relationships in popular love songs is either omitted entirely, or only implied in a way that is hidden from view. In the Top 40 what is usually hidden is that the love relationship implied by the lyrics is often partially or entirely disconnected (alienation).

Connectedness with others (solidarity or attunement), along with its opposite, alienation, are fundamental ideas in social science; connectedness is a basic human need in all times and places. Connection with others has many names; it is sometimes referred to as cohesion or trust. Social connection is as necessary as the air we breathe; it is social oxygen. One implication of this idea is that even if lack of connection is hidden or ignored, a terrible price will ultimately be paid. Similarly, the social science of emotions proposes that not coming to terms with one's emotions causes problems without end.

The main concern of this book is to help readers understand the emotions and relationships portrayed in popular lyrics to the point that they can better understand themselves and their own relationships. Even though our educational system hardly ever touches on this kind of learning, it is nevertheless extremely important to help students in this area.

ACKNOWLEDGMENTS

This book could not have been written without the help of students over a long period of time: Max Anders, Mairead Donahey, Erica Kraschinsky, Byron Miller, Lindsey Koro, Margaret Retsch, Lauren Tokushige, Jacob Goren, and many more, and advice from Dean Birkenkamp, Robert Fuller, Suzanne Retzinger, and Julie Scheff. This book is dedicated to my many helpers and advisors, named and unnamed.

CHAPTER 1

INTRODUCTION

What's in a Love Song?

There is a large scholarly literature on popular songs, but most of the writers only discuss very general and abstract ideas. Many essays have made the point that popular love songs are not like real love. But they don't go on to point out clearly how they differ. Similarly, the idea that popular songs matter because they evoke emotions is also not new. Most observers of popular music agree.

For example, Simon Frith, perhaps the leading scholar of popular music, makes this point repeatedly in "Why Do Songs Have Words?" (2007, 209–239) in his book *Taking Popular Music Seriously*. However, neither Frith nor any other scholars consider specific emotions. They are discussed only in the abstract, making the comments almost meaningless. This book explores specific emotions, such as love, genuine pride, grief, anger, and others, in the hope of clarifying the meaning that popular songs have for their audience.

Three questions about emotions in popular songs require exploration: 1. How do these lyrics define the emotion of love?

2. How are other emotions represented or distorted in the lyrics?
3. What kinds of lyrics would help, rather than hinder, the listener's development as a person in the real world?

The '50s song "That's Amore" provides an extreme example of one way of defining love: "When the moon hits your eye / Like a big-a pizza pie / That's amore." This lyric is probably the champion of goofiness, but it appears that most other popular lyrics seldom provide realistic definitions either.

The meaning of love has been hotly debated for thousands of years, and continues to be. One of the many divisive issues is whether love is ineffable, a mystery, the less talked about, the better. The "big-a pizza" lyric and many others contribute to maintaining the mystery, since they reveal next to nothing about the look and feel of actual love.

On another side of the debate there has been a call for realistic descriptions. This book proposes that since most popular songs help preserve the mystery, we also need realistic approaches if we are to understand the meaning of these songs, much less real love itself. As already indicated, this first chapter introduces the debate on the meaning of love, and the sixth chapter describes and defines both romantic and non-erotic (family) love.

What are the pleasures and pains of love? A French folk song is eloquent on this topic:

> The joys of love
> Are but a moment long
> The pain of love endures
> A whole life long. ("Plaisir d'Amour")

This lyric is blunt to the point of despair: the pleasures of love are brief, the pains are forever. Although overstating the case, the implication that love is a mixture of pleasure and pain counters the tendency in popular songs toward idealization and fantasy. This lyric doesn't quite involve another aspect of the question, however: the intensity of the pleasures and pains. Popular songs speak to both aspects in loud voices. Most lyrics about the earliest stages of love suggest that the pleasures are virtually infinite. Songs about the later stages, especially those about *heartbreak*, the loss of love, usually imply that the pain is not only of long duration, but also intense to the point of being unbearable.

Understanding how popular songs portray the meaning of love and its pain/pleasure turns out to be more complex than one would first think. What we understand depends on how we define love and other emotions, not a simple task. In some ways, the questions asked here are just different sides of the same coin. The pains and pleasures of love that we identify depend largely on how we define love and the emotions that usually accompany it.

Popular songs overwhelmingly define the emotion of love broadly and loosely. The "big-a pizza" lyric is only one of many instances. For one thing, most include "falling in love," even with a person that one has only seen at a distance. This kind of "love" brings up the question of whether one can love a person one doesn't know. In the English language, at least, one can even love an inanimate object—red wine, old farmhouses—so why not a person who is entirely a mystery? In English, love is frequent and cheap, at least more than in all other languages.

Popular love songs also take other liberties. For example, they take the intensity of the pain of heartbreak as a measure of love: the more intense and longer lasting the pain of loss, the greater the love. Alternative possibilities will be discussed later. Love in popular song lyrics can also mean many different kinds of feeling, not only affection and sexual desire, but also infatuation and sexual desire without affection. It can also mean loving someone that you don't even like. In order to get a better understanding of romance as described in popular songs, and even as it is lived in real life, a clearer understanding of the meaning of genuine love might be helpful.

It appears that the English language defines love much more loosely than other languages. There are two different Top 40s in Spanish, one in Spain and one in Latin America. The same patterns of meanings are found in both, but the number of lyrics that can be classified as requited love is somewhat larger than in the English language lyrics. There also seem to be fewer liberties taken with the meaning of love, although there are many popular lyrics that toy with different terms for love. Still it would seem that the Spanish language is less loose with the meaning of love than English.

The second question that drives this book: what other emotions besides love can be identified in popular lyrics? This book considers the language of emotion used in popular love songs in the United States over a period of seventy-eight years (1930–2008). In some ways the language of emotion is fairly transparent, but in other ways it is shockingly ambiguous and confusing. We've already discussed the extremely broad meaning of love as it is described in lyrics. Another problem might be called the enigma of the missing emotions. The emotions frequently represented in Top 40 love lyrics are fairly obvious, but some are only hinted at. This issue is especially relevant to popular songs about heartbreak.

Love songs by far dominate the Top 40, and heartbreak lyrics have long been the single largest category. At least for the period 1930–2000, 25 percent of the U.S. Top 40 concern the pain of losing one's beloved. Songs about requited love, on the one hand,

and infatuation, on the other, also appear repeatedly, but much less frequently than heartbreak; each of these other topics involves less than ten percent of the Top 40. Finally, there is always a miscellaneous group that includes many kinds of issues, such as explicit sexuality and comedy. Although the content of the miscellaneous category of Top 40 love lyrics has changed somewhat over the last 80 years, the proportion has remained the same, at about 17 percent.

However, one substantial change has occurred in the miscellaneous category, especially over the last ten years: the appearance of many sexually explicit lyrics. Largely due to the influence of rap and hip hop, most of the sexual lyrics eliminate any thought of commitment to a relationship. Indeed, some don't even award respect to the other person. The masculine lyrics, particularly, are degrading to women. Since these songs take the love out of romance, they might be fairly considered to be anti-love songs.

Emotions That Accompany the Emotion of Love

Here are some representative heartbreak lyrics in which the representation of emotions other than love is fairly transparent. They all involve an extreme situation, loss of the loved one, usually because of rejection. Less extreme situations, such as those that don't involve complete loss and/or rejection, are seldom considered. Popular love songs aim for the highly dramatic, rather than the long haul. Emotional pain within requited love, for example, is virtually unknown.

Many heartbreak songs are straightforwardly about the kind of complete and dramatic loss that gives rise to intense *grief*.

So I drown myself with tears,

Sittin' here, singin' another sad love song ("Lately" 1998)

As is the case with most heartbreak lyrics, this one doesn't actually mention grief, the emotion of loss. Yet the reference is clear because of the prominence of tears and sadness, as in this song also:

Girl, each time I try I just break down and cry

...

Oh, I'd rather be dead ... ("End of the Road" 1992)

The last line, particularly, is of interest, because like many heartbreak lyrics, it implies that the pain of loss is so great as to be unbearable. As already mentioned, this unending battle with pain is usually assumed to register the depth of love. An alternative interpretation is that it might only imply the inability to work through the pain of loss in order to get on with one's life. Often portrayals of love and loss seem closer to obsessional neurosis than to real love. This could be a serious matter, since the lyrics seem to confirm the impossibility of resolving grief.

The continuing, overwhelming presence of the pain of loss and rejection is emphasized in the following lyric. The ironic and somewhat playful tone is unusual. The first few lines of this song convey a feeling of sadness yet acceptance. However, the two lines below are from the chorus and they represent sadness only.

And it only hurts when I'm breathing

My heart only breaks when it's beating

("It Only Hurts When I'm Breathing" 2004)

This lyric also refers, playfully and therefore indirectly, to another prominent theme in heartbreak lyrics, what might be called the curtailment of feeling (Chapter 5). In this particular lyric, curtailment is only hinted at through irony. As will be noted in Chapter 5, the curtailment of feeling in Top 40 lyrics was generalized and abstract between 1930 and 1958. After 1958, it became dominant, detailed, and intense.

This is an excerpt from another lyric that focuses on continuous pain by a detailed review of the events of a whole day, from awaking in the morning to sleep at night (abbreviated):

> I'm half alive but I feel mostly dead
> I try and tell myself it'll be all right
> ("You Were Meant for Me" 1996)

The last lyric is unusually concrete in describing the details of constant pain. The overall theme of the songs is mourning the loss of a lover. As indicated by the line "I'm half alive but I feel mostly dead," the pain of loss is represented as infinite.

A second type of heartbreak lyric also implies grief, but includes *anger* as well, even though the anger is represented somewhat indirectly:

> Could you cry a little
> ...
> Pretend that you're feeling a little more pain ("Cry" 2002)

The desire for revenge, wanting the lost lover to feel pain also, is a manifestation of anger. The implication that the lover lies and only pretends to care is another indication of blame and anger.

Anger and revenge are also implied in this lyric:

> Someday I'm gonna run across your mind
> ...

> I'll be over you and on with my life
> ("You'll Think of Me" 2002)

The hint of revenge is muffled: "Someday I'm gonna run across your mind ... While you're sleeping with your pride." The implication seems to be that the lost lover may someday feel the pain of loss, no matter how faintly, that the singer is feeling.

Many heartbreak songs imply anger through sarcasm. An obvious example is the Bob Dylan classic "Don't Think Twice, It's All Right":

> You just kinda wasted my precious time
> But don't think twice, it's all right.

The sarcasm of this lyric implies not only anger, but also, like "It Only Hurts When I'm Breathing," mentioned above, curtailment of feeling, since the anger is expressed indirectly through sarcasm. Although the majority of Top 40 heartbreak lyrics refer to grief alone, many also include anger, if only indirectly.

Hidden Emotions

There are still other kinds of emotion implied in addition to grief and anger.

The following lyric implies the emotion of grief ("crying inside"), but also refers to a highly abstract and generalized feeling ("pain"). It is quite explicit and raw, however, about curtailment:

> The pain is real even if nobody knows
> Now I'm cryin' inside

("Nobody Knows" 1996).

The following lyric also refers to grief (sad, tears), but it also introduces another highly abstract emotion word, "hurt:"

> Cos really I'm sad, Oh I'm sadder than sad
> Well I'm hurt and I want you so bad
> ("Tears of a Clown" 1968)

The only direct indications of emotion are grief (crying inside, sad and sadness). They are used, however, to imply not only grief but the pain of rejection. What is the emotion of rejection? It is pictured as doubly painful, since, like many heartbreak lyrics, it implies that rejection is exquisitely painful in itself and also requires hiding it from others, introducing a second kind of pain.

Although this kind of emotional pain tied to rejection is quite common in heartbreak lyrics, most students I have asked are unable to provide a specific name for it. It is clearly distinct from the four emotions that have been mentioned so far, love, grief, anger, and pride. It is obviously not joy or pride. Could it be fear or shame? No fair using the term "hurt" because it includes many kinds of emotional pain. What would you call it? Don't worry if you can't identify it; the problem of the emotion that is the shadow of love will be discussed in Chapter 7.

Some new issues arise from the problems discussed above. The first is, why is it that there is so little agreement about defining love? The second, how should we name the emotion of rejection? To prepare to discuss these questions, the second chapter considers the problem of naming emotions, not just in song lyrics, but in the English language in general. Because of this link, the conclusions drawn from identifying emotions in popular song lyrics may have implications for the world of real emotions in which we live.

Emotions Provide Value in the Universe of Thought and Beliefs

Our society teaches us that it is the outside world, behavior, and thought that are important, not the inner life of emotions. Yet this orientation can be misleading. Since this issue is so fundamental, some space must be given to it.

Experts agree that emotion and feeling are important for many reasons. However, there may be a reason so far little mentioned that is concerned with cognition: emotions can serve to distinguish what is important to the individual from myriads of cognitions that are not (see Nussbaum 2001 for an argument that takes a different path but ends with a similar conclusion).

This idea can be illustrated by some of the visitors to an Iraq War Memorial installed on Sundays by the Veterans for Peace (Scheff 2007). It is set up on the beach alongside the Santa Barbara pier: more than four thousand crosses representing U.S. military deaths in Iraq. It looks like a cemetery the size of a football field, clearly visible to car and pedestrian traffic on the pier. Most don't stop to look, much less talk, even though the memorial is impossible to miss, being immediately adjacent to the right side of the pier. Even automobile passengers can see it when driving out to the end of the pier.

Almost all tourists, they are on the pier for pleasure. The great majority don't seem to know or care that they are passing by a memorial. But a small percentage, perhaps one in ten, stop to look. Of these, half seek more information.

Most who stop are puzzled. Like the other members of VFP on duty at the pier, I try to answer their questions. They are surprised and shocked when they understand what it is they are seeing. Women often cry, and men look sad and may make a donation, sometimes a sizable one. Most say "I didn't know so many had died," or "Before I saw this, it was just a number to me." The physical size of the memorial has overwhelmed their defenses against the painful feeling of loss.

The implication is that now it is not just a number, because it now connects with strong feeling. In order to get through the day, we all carry a vast baggage of cognitions. Modern societies require everyone to know a colossal number of words, phrases, facts, and factoids. In addition to what is required, each person also carries his or her own personal mass of thoughts and memories. Most have no meaning at all, being "just a number/thought/memory," etc. Emotions and feelings, even weak ones, serve as tags for what is significant. The visitors to the war memorial already knew that a large number of U.S. soldiers had died in Iraq, but until they *felt* its meaning, it was just one of many meaningless numbers.

Unlike the intergalactic universe of cognitions, the domain of emotion and feeling is quite small. There may be only a dozen or so true emotions, culturally universal, genetically determined states of bodily arousal (such as love, joy, fear, grief, anger, contempt, disgust, pride, and shame). There are more affects, emotion and cognition combinations, with the emotion part strong (jealousy, vengefulness, etc.), say fifty. Finally there is a still larger domain of feelings, also a cognition/emotion combination, but with the emotion component weak, often a mere tinge (e.g., nostalgia). Perhaps there are hundreds of these.

But compared to the "numberless infinity" (John Donne's phrase) of cognitions, even a tinge of emotion may be enough to provide force and significance. *Without emotions, we would all be adrift in an endless ocean of thoughts and memories,* most of them holding little or no meaning. The mind, as we say, is free, but also extraordinarily crowded. For most people, most of the time, emotions serve as the markers that bequeath value, virtually all value. Needless to say, there are exceptions. Scientific formulae and systems have a value largely independent of emotions, at least for scientists. But in the everyday world for most people, most of the time, value and significance are generated by emotions, even in the mundane life of scientists.

Emotions point us toward meaning in our lives. However, in modern societies, spontaneous emotions are systematically discouraged, both in children and in adults. As already mentioned, they are curtailed. Boys, especially, quickly learn that emotions other than anger are usually taken as a sign of weakness. Women in the workplace know that crying is unlikely to be tolerated. Recent medical research on emotions treats them as the enemy. Not only bouts of anger, but also fear, grief, and shame may be diagnosed as Emotional Lability (EL), or a more extreme label, "Emotional Incontinence." Perhaps such terms should make us thankful for the diagnostic label of alexithymia (emotionlessness), which is probably far more widespread than too much emotion.

The intolerance of authentic emotions and mass hypercognition together may be the main reason that the need for meaning can be exploited. In mass entertainment, popular music and commercial films usually follow mechanical formulas that arouse emotions. Most popular songs attract attention not because of their art, but because they manipulate unresolved emotions, especially romantic feelings and grief. Horror films, similarly, arouse fear. Action films both arouse and justify the emotion of anger (righteous anger) and the affect of vengeance. Mass entertainment seems to be popular to the extent that it arouses emotions, no matter how mechanically.

The fact that popular songs arouse emotion, however mechanically, is probably the main reason they are so excruciatingly important for so many people. Popular love songs offer one of the few arenas charged with intense emotions. Certainly our educational system offers very little in the way of strong emotions, or even any emotions at all. Especially during the years in which I worked on this book, I found that many college students hold popular songs in awe, like a religion.

Political exploitation of the need for meaning through emotion may be a similar device. The fraudulent marketing of the Iraq war was probably successful because it played on and amplified the fear and vengefulness in the public that resulted from 9/11. Perhaps manipulation of the public will continue as long as authentic emotions are lost in a sea of cognition.

Types of Relationships

There is another dimension of popular love songs that is just as important as the emotions represented: the types of relationships implied. This dimension is virtually never alluded to directly, but is always present in one way or another.

In the English language, the quality of relationships is not easy to describe. One way that is available is the difference between friendships, business or professional relationships, and familial patterns, such as marriage, parent-child, or siblings. But these terms tell us next to nothing about relationship quality.

The quality of a relationship seems to be a function of the degree of *connectedness*, of mutual understanding. Defining genuine love will depend on this idea. It will turn out to be the second dimension of the quality of relationships in lyrics, not just the types of emotions implied, but also the degree of mutual understanding. Closeness always seems to involve mutual understanding, and alienation lack of it.

One complication of alienation is that it can come in two different and opposing forms: being too far apart (isolation), or being too close (engulfment or dependency). This latter type of alienation involves giving up parts of self out of loyalty to the other. It is a kind of alienation or estrangement from self. A further complication involves not only the degree of mutual understanding between the lover and the beloved, but also the relationship implied between them and the larger world. As it turns out, many lyrics, especially recent ones, suggest alienation from the larger community, us against them, like Bonnie and Clyde. This latter theme will be further discussed in the last chapter.

Most popular love songs imply one or more of these various types of relationships. Describing both the emotions represented and the types of relationships provides a detailed portrait of the social-emotional world represented in popular songs.

Conclusion

This book proposes that, with only a few exceptions, popular love songs legitimatize and help generate the dysfunctional responses to our emotions and dysfunctional types of relationships that are the norm in our society. The song that gives this book its title, "What's Love Got to Do with It?" (1984) may have a point: "Love is a second-hand emotion." That is, love as represented in popular songs is just an endless rerun of the dysfunctional way the word is used in our society. How could this pattern be changed? The last chapter addresses this question.

For sake of discussion, suppose we assume that the conclusions drawn about emotions and relationships in popular songs are applicable to the real world. What are the implications for interpersonal and societal relationships at large? In particular, can we identify the actual emotions and relationships underlying infatuation, love, and heartbreak as a first step toward understanding? Which brings us to the third and final question: *What kinds of love songs would help us understand love, rather than confuse and complicate it?* Some classic popular lyrics that illustrate remedies for the pains of love will be offered.

In the next chapter, a theory of the linkages between emotions and relationships will be proposed. It suggests that most emotions arise out of relationship events, and that the structure of relationships, in turn, is in some ways parallel to the structure of emotional experiences. This proposal amounts to a theory of the social-emotional world that will be helpful in understanding lyrics, and possibly in changing them.

CHAPTER 2

CONCEPTIONS OF LOVE

The Eternal Debate

What is this thing called love?
This funny thing called love?

This lyric from 1929 catches an important note about love in modern societies, its mystery and magic. If love can be defined, should it be? This book will argue that we need to define love carefully if we are to understand popular song lyrics, and more importantly, ourselves and our society.

The first step toward defining love will be to refer to the large literature on this topic, the way in which classic and contemporary scholars have conceptualized love. I begin with vernacular meanings of love. If love is defined so broadly in modern societies as to be virtually meaningless, how can we rescue its meaning?

Before proceeding, it should be said that investigating love might seem to be subversive. Any study of the fundamentals of a society could challenge assumptions that are taken for granted in everyday life. As we go about our daily activities, we have neither the interest nor the resources to check on the thousands of assumptions that we make, and to a large extent, share with other members of our society. Just getting through the day is enough of a challenge.

Only eccentrics, artists, or scientists have the time and inclination to challenge everyday assumptions. Erving Goffman's work, for example, partakes of all three of these worlds: eccentricity, art, and science. The most common criticisms of his writing are that it is bitter, cynical, or sour. The charges, for the most part, seem to arise out of his challenge to our taken-for-granted assumptions. Any sustained investigation of the social-emotional world might challenge major institutions; not only the political and economic ones, but also those dealing with family, education, religion, and the cult of individualism in modern societies.

One of the central ideas in this book is that a total individualism is taken for granted in Western societies. Our "common sense," the shared understandings we have in these societies, tells us to focus on individuals, rather than relationships. Another set of assumptions concerns which emotions are good and which are bad.

In this chapter, I suggest that the emotion of love is seen as good, and is used, therefore, as often as possible. This assumption is groundless, of course, since love in itself is neither good nor bad, or better yet, it is both good and bad. Love can be experienced in different modes, some very painful. Increasing our understanding of love, step by step, to the extent that it brings out these various shades of love may also challenge our taken-for-granted assumptions about ourselves, the people in our lives, and our relationships with them.

Current Usage

One obvious cause for confusion is the many ways the word *love* is used in Western societies. According to Harold Bloom (1998, 549), Aldous Huxley suggested "we use the word love for the most amazing variety of relationships, ranging from what we feel for our mothers to what we feel for someone we beat up in a bordello, or its many equivalents."[1]

The comment about beating someone up out of love is probably not an exaggeration. A set of experiments suggests that subjects' condemnation of murder is softened if they are told that it was caused by jealousy (Puente and Cohen 2003). These subjects seem to entertain the idea that one can love someone so much that one kills them, loving them to death.

Solomon (1981, 3–4) elaborates on the broad sweep of the word *love*:

> Consider ... the wealth of meticulous and fine distinctions we make in describing our feelings of hostility: hatred, loathing, scorn, anger, revulsion, resentment, envy, abhorrence, malice, aversion, vexation, irritation, annoyance, disgust, spite and contempt, or worse, "beneath" contempt. And yet we sort out our positive affections for the most part between the two limp categories, "liking" and "loving." We distinguish our friends from mere acquaintances and make a ready distinction between lovers and friends whom we love "but not that way." Still, one and the same word serves to describe our enthusiasm for apple strudel, respect for a distant father, the anguish of an uncertain romantic affair and nostalgic affection for an old pair of slippers ...

Solomon (1981, 7) goes on to quote Voltaire: "There are so many sorts of love that one does not know where to seek a definition of it." In modern societies the broad use of the word *love* may defend against the painful absence of true intimacy and community. The idea seems to be that ANY kind of relationship that has positive elements in it, even if mixed with extremely negative ones, can be called love.

What Does Love Mean?

One place to seek definitions is the dictionary. The English language unabridged dictionaries provide some *two dozen* meanings for love (TWO DOZEN!), most of them applicable to romantic or close relationships. These are the first two meanings in the American Heritage Dictionary (1992):

1. A deep, tender, ineffable feeling of affection and solicitude toward a person, such as that arising from kinship, recognition of attractive qualities, or a sense of underlying oneness.

2. A feeling of intense desire and attraction toward a person with whom one is disposed to make a pair; the emotion of sex and romance.

These two definitions are of great interest, because they touch upon several complexities. Particularly daunting is the idea that love is ineffable (indescribable). I can sympathize with this idea because genuine love seems to be quite complex. Both popular and scholarly accounts flirt with the idea that one of the crowning qualities of love is that it is mysterious and therefore indescribable. Nevertheless, this chapter will attempt to summarize some of love's features as described by dictionaries, scholars, and other writers.

The first dictionary definition (above) is very broad, covering both romantic and other kinds of love, such as love of kin or friends. The second is narrower, involving only romantic love and emphasizing sexual attraction. Of the twenty or so remaining definitions, a few are unrelated to relationships (such as the use of the word *love* in scoring a tennis match). Most of them, however, involve various shadings and gradations of love, and especially, of romantic love. Given the many possible meanings of the word, it is no wonder that scholars and, more recently, social scientists seem so divided on its significance.

Of all the basic emotions, love is the least clearly defined. Our conceptions of anger, fear, shame, grief, contempt, disgust, and joy are fuzzy around the edges, but they are clear enough so that we can begin to communicate about them. At the most elementary level, we feel we are able at least to distinguish between painful emotions, such as fear, grief, and shame, and pleasurable ones, like interest, excitement, and joy.

But about love, particularly romantic love, there is little agreement. Even on so basic an issue as whether love is painful or pleasurable, experts are divided. Indeed, reading the scholarly literature, it often seems that they are not talking about the same emotion. Some experts, both classical and modern, consider love not only pleasurable, but in many ways the most important thing in life. Nevertheless, this view represents only a minority. The dominant view has long been that love, especially romantic love, is a painful affliction or madness, a view widely held by the ancient Greeks (De Rougement 1940). Over 2500 years ago, Sappho described the pain and impairment of love.

> For should I see thee a little moment,
> Straight my voice is hushed;

> Yea, my tongue is broken, and
> Through me
> 'Neath the flesh, impalpable fire
> Runs tingling;
> Nothing sees mine eyes, and a
> Voice of roaring
> Waves in my ear sounds;
> Sweat runs down in rivers, a
> Tremor seize
> All my limbs, and paler than
> Grass in autumn,
> Caught by pains of menacing
> Death, I falter,
> Lost in the love-trance.

Certainly in the teachings of the Church Fathers, beginning with St. Augustine, romantic love has been viewed as a disorder because of the sinfulness of sexuality. The eleventh century scholar Andreas Capellanas (*The Art of Courtly Love* 1969), after an extended indictment of romantic love, concluded that it was the work of the Devil.

The majority of secular scholars have also taken the position that romantic love is an affliction or madness. The most elaborate description of romantic love is found in Stendhal's *Love* (1975). Although he denies that passionate love is pathological, he inconsistently acknowledges that it is a disease. Certainly his description emphasizes the painful rather than the pleasurable aspects. At the beginning, one is lost in obsession:

> The most surprising thing of all about love is the first step, the violence of the change that takes place in the mind.... A person in

love is unremittingly and uninterruptedly occupied with the image of the beloved.

In the later stages, Stendhal notes, many other surprises await, most of them unpleasant: "Then you reach the final torment: utter despair poisoned still further by a shred of hope." Although Stendhal included positive aspects of love, the philosopher Ortega y Gasset saw only the negative (*On Love* 1957), calling romantic love an abnormality. This passage suggests the flavor of his critique:

> The soul of a man in love smells of the closed-up room of a sick man—its confined atmosphere is filled with stale breath.

Even Freud, a champion of sexuality, saw romantic love negatively. He commented that falling in love was a kind of "sickness and craziness, an illusion, a blindness to what the loved person is really like" (Freud 1915). Here he seems to equate love with infatuation, a topic I will take up below.

On the other hand, to give Freud credit, he also saw the positive side of love, at least of non-erotic love. When Jung challenged him to name the curative aspect of psychoanalysis, Freud answered very simply, "Love." This answer is very much in harmony with the definition of love that will be offered in this chapter.

Modern scholarship is more evenly divided between positive and negative views than classical discussions. Hatfield and Rapson (1993) distinguish between passionate love (infatuation) and companionate love (fondness). Both Solomon (1992) and Sternberg (1988) distinguish between love and infatuation. They note that both involve intense desire, but that love also involves intimacy and commitment. Kemper and Reid (1997) also distinguish between what they call "adulation" and what they see as later stages, ideal and romantic love. Like Persons (1988), they seem to assume that beginning with infatuation is likely to lead on to love. However, infatuation can also lead to more infatuation, either with the same or different persons. For Solomon and for Sternberg, love is highly positive and complex; it is infatuation that is simple and negative. As we shall see, this distinction may be too crude. But, if refined, it could be one step toward the development of a workable concept of love.

Soble (1990) provides a summary of the many components of the meaning of love, such as the uniqueness of the beloved, how the beloved comes first, satisfies desire, is exclusive and constant, and provides reciprocity. His account is historical, however, rather than analytic.

Another detailed analysis of the meaning of the word *love* in English is provided by Johnson (2001). He shows that the vernacular word implies three different kinds of love: care, desire for union, or appreciation. These three forms, he argues, may exist independently or in combination. One limitation of his approach is that it does not include the physical component of love, attachment. Another is that it is atheoretical, in that it is based entirely on vernacular usage in the English language. Although it is useful to have such detailed treatments, it still leaves the analysis of the meaning of love located completely in only one culture. Nor does either book propose a single overarching definition.

Kemper (1978) analyzed the way in which social relationships generate love as well as other emotions, in terms of status and power. The awarding of status, which is crucial in Kemper's theory, will be important here also, since it is an aspect of shared identity. Power, however, does not seem to be involved in love as defined here, since shared identity means its absence. Although I agree that most emotions arise out of relationship dynamics, Kemper's theory seems to deal only partially with shared identity, and not at all with attachment, attraction, and empathic resonance (attunement).

Perhaps the best empirical study of romantic love, and certainly the most detailed, is by Tennov (1979), who interviewed hundreds of persons about their romantic life. She found that the great majority of her subjects had frequently experienced the trance of love, like the one in Sappho's poem. However, Tennov does not call this state *love* or even *infatuation*. Instead she uses the word "limerance," which refers to a trance-like state. Perhaps aware of the many ambiguities in the way the word *love* is used, Tennov seems to have wanted a neutral term, rather than the usual one.

The conflict between the different points of view described above is the result, for the most part, of the broad sweep covered by the word *love*. The arguments are a confusion of meanings, since the various sides are referring to different affects. Those who see romantic love as pathological are considering the affect that I prefer to call infatuation and/or the sex drive, without considering other aspects of what is called love. This usage is perfectly proper in English and French (but not in Spanish). Most references to "falling in love" or "love at first sight" concern infatuation. With regard to lust, recall that one of the dictionary definitions of love is "A feeling of intense desire and attraction toward a person with whom one is disposed to make a pair; the emotion of sex and romance," which is entirely about sexual desire.

On the other hand, those authors that stress the positive aspects of love focus on the emotional and relational aspects, companionship and caring. I will consider these aspects under the heading of "attunement," the sharing of identity and awareness between persons in love. As should become clear in this chapter, this is only one part of love, even non-erotic love. Perhaps there will be less conflict and confusion if we can agree on a definition of love that is less vague and broad than vernacular usage.

Three Components of Love

The social science literature on love is divided into three separate schools of thought. The first school focuses on biology. This school holds that *attachment*, a genetically endowed physical phenomenon, is the basis for non-erotic love. The second school considers only romantic love, and focuses only on sexual attraction. The idea that the dominant force in love is attachment and/or sexual attraction is stated explicitly by Shaver and Clark (1994), Shackelflord (1998), Fisher (1992), and many others. This idea has strong connections with evolutionary theory, proposing that love is a mammalian drive, like hunger and thirst.

A further frisson for these two schools of thought has been provided by discussions of limbic communication (Lewis et al. 2000). According to this work, persons in physically close quarters develop physiologically based resonance, body to body. One striking example they cite concerns women roommates whose menstrual cycles gradually move toward the same date of the month. Lewis and his colleagues urge bodily resonance as the dominant component in love. They also explicitly link it to attachment theory (idem, pp. 69–76). From this point of view, love is a constant and a universal, from individual to individual, in all cultures and historical times.

Various studies both of humans and animals have suggested that attachment is primarily based on the close relationship of infants to their caretakers. Infants imprint on one or both parents, and anyone else in close and continued proximity. Although not all of the causes of imprinting have been established, touch, body warmth, and the sense of smell are prime candidates. Several studies suggest that an infant will select its own mother's milk over the milk produced by other mothers, probably based on smell. This smell may be carried with us as long as we live, even if only far below the level of conscious awareness. As adults, we may still become attached to others because of their smell, even if we don't realize it. But there may be other roads to attachment, as will be discussed below.

There is a third major school of thought, however, that gives little or no attention to a physical basis for love. This school proposes that love is largely a psychological/emotional/cultural phenomenon. In this perspective, love is seen as extremely variable and changeable, by individuals, social classes, and/or cultures and historical epochs.

Most of this chapter will be devoted to this idea—not because the first two ideas are unimportant. In the scheme of things, the physical bases of love are just as important as the cultural/cognitive/emotional one. My attention will focus mainly on the latter idea because it is much more subtle, complex, and counterintuitive than the first. It is also a component that is more susceptible to intentional change than attachment and attraction.

Attachment and sexual attraction are relatively simple, constant, and universal in all cultures and historical periods. They are built into the human body, as they are built into the bodies of other mammals. They can vary in intensity, and in the degree to which they are expressed or inhibited, but they are basically one-dimensional. Not so with the cultural/cognitive/emotional component, which has many dimensions, ramifications, and contradictions.

Love as Mutual Identity

By far the most sophisticated version of the third perspective is proposed by the philosopher Robert Solomon (1976, 1981, 1994). There are many features of Solomon's treatment of love that distinguish it from other writings. First, his analysis of love is conceptual and comparative: in his treatments, he examines love in the context of a similar examination of other emotions. The way in which he compared the broadness of the meaning of love with the specificity of anger words, quoted above, is illustrative of his approach. Indeed, his first analysis of love occurred in a volume in which he gave more or less equal space to the other major emotions (*The Passions* 1976). Locating love with respect to other emotions is extremely important, since many of the classical and modern discussions get lost in the uniqueness, and therefore the ineffability, of love.

A second feature of his approach is that he provides a broad picture of the effects of emotion on the person undergoing them, in addition to the central feeling. He calls this broad summary "the emotionworld." For example, he compares the "loveworld" to the "angerworld." The loveworld (Solomon 1981, 126) is "woven around a single relationship, with everything else pushed to the periphery ... " By contrast, he states, in the angerworld "one defines oneself in the role of the 'offended' and someone else.... as the 'offender.' [It] is very much a courtroom world, a world filled with blame and emotional litigation ... " Solomon uses the skills of a novelist to try to convey the experience of emotion, including cognition and perception, not just the sensation or the outward appearance.

From my point of view, however, Solomon's most important contribution is his definition of the central feature of love as *shared identity* (Solomon 1981, xxx; 1994, 235): " ... love [is] shared identity, a redefinition of self which no amount of sex or fun or time together will add up to.... Two people in a society with an extraordinary sense of individual identity mutually fantasize, verbalize and act their way into a relationship that can no longer be understood as a mere conjunction of the two but only as a complex ONE."

By locating love in the larger perceptual/behavioral framework, and by comparing love with other emotions, Solomon manages both to evoke love as an emotion and develop a concrete description of its causes, appearance, and effects, a significant achievement. His work suggests that the reason scholars decide that love is ineffable is because they treat it that way, a self-fulfilling prophecy that Solomon avoids.

At first sight, Solomon's deconstruction of the concept of love may appear to be Grinch-like. Why remove the aura of ineffability, of sacred mystery by means of comparison with other emotions, by locating feelings within a larger framework of perceptions and behavior, and by invoking a general concept like shared identity? Perhaps this attempt is only one more example of what Max Weber called the progressive disenchantment of the world.

This is an important issue; we cannot afford just to shrug it off. Perhaps it is the price one has to pay for the advancement of understanding. But there is a further reason that is less obvious, that the broad use of the word *love* is a defense against painful feelings of separation and alienation. People who go around proclaiming their love for others, as in the farewell "Love ya," may be running on empty. It is possible that the way that the idea of love evokes positive feelings of awe and mystery is also a defense against painful feelings of separation and alienation.

In any event, this chapter seeks to extend Solomon's conceptualization of love as an emotion like other emotions. Solomon's idea that genuine love involves a union between the lovers is not new. It is found, as he suggests, in Plato and Aristotle. It also appears in one of Shakespeare's riddling poems about love, "The Phoenix and the Turtle," as in this stanza:

> Property was thus appall'd,
> That the self was not the same;
> Single nature's double name
> Neither two nor one was call'd.

The idea of unity is also alluded to in the first dictionary definition, quoted above, as "a sense of ... oneness," and in many other conceptions of the nature of love. In current discussion, the idea of unity is referred to as connectedness, shared awareness, intersubjectivity, or attunement.

Love and Solidarity

Any theory of social integration, like attachment theory, assumes that humanness requires being connected to others. There is a vast literature supporting the idea that all humans have a need to belong (Baumeister and Leary 1995). Love is one form of belonging; friendship and community are two other forms. But in modern societies these kinds of needs are difficult to fulfill. Infatuation, heartbreak, and on a larger scale, blind patriotism offer a substitute: imagining and longing for an ideal person or group instead of connecting with a real one. (In his treatise on the psychological bases of nationalism, Anderson [1991] calls the nation "an imagined community.")

One complication involved with the idea of the need for connectedness is that humans, unlike other mammals, also have a strong need for individual and group autonomy. These two needs are equal and opposite. The clash between needs for both connection and autonomy forms the backdrop for cooperation and conflict between individuals and also between groups. I will return to the issue of autonomy in the discussion of micro-solidarity and micro-alienation below.

The idea of a connection between two persons is difficult to make explicit in Western societies because of the strong focus on individuals, rather than relationships or connectedness between persons. The idea of connectedness implies that humans, unlike other creatures, can share the experience of another. That is, that a part of individual consciousness is not only subjective, but also intersubjective.

The idea of an intersubjective component in consciousness has been mentioned many times in the history of philosophy, but the implications are seldom explored. The early American sociologist C. H. Cooley argued that intersubjectivity is so much a part of the humanness of human nature that most of us take it completely for granted, to the point of invisibility.

Cooley's idea that we are "living in the minds of others without knowing it" is profoundly significant for understanding the cognitive component of love (Cooley 1922, 177). Intersubjectivity is so built into our humanness that it will usually be virtually invisible. It follows that we should expect most people have learned to ignore clues that point toward intersubjectivity.

This element is what Stern (1977) has called attunement (mutual understanding). John Dewey proposed that attunement formed the core of communication: "Shared experience is the greatest of human goods. In communication, such conjunction and contact as is characteristic of animals become endearments capable of infinite idealization; they become symbols of the very culmination of nature" (Dewey 1925, 202).

In ordinary language, attunement involves connectedness between people, deep and seemingly effortless understanding, and understanding that one is understood. As already indicated, this idea is hinted at in that part of the dictionary definition about "a sense of ... oneness."

In order to visualize intersubjectivity, it may be necessary to take this idea a step further than Cooley did in his idea of the looking-glass self by thinking of it more concretely. How does it actually work in dialogue? One recent suggestion that may be helpful is the idea of "pendulation," that interacting with others, we swing back and forth between our own point of view and that of the other (Levine 1997). It is this back and forth movement between subjective and intersubjective consciousness that allows mutual understanding.

The infinite ambiguity of ordinary human language makes intersubjectivity a necessity for communication. The signs and gestures used by non-human creatures are completely unambiguous. For example, bees can instantly detect the smell of strange bees: it signals enemy. But humans can easily hide their feelings and intentions under deceitful or ambiguous messages. Even with the best intentions, communications in ordinary language are inherently ambiguous, because all ordinary words are allowed many meanings, depending on the context. Understanding even fairly simple messages requires mutual role-taking (attunement) because the meaning of messages is dependent on the context.

As suggested, any context can easily change the meaning of any message. To understand the meaning of messages in context, we have all become adroit at pendulation: seeing the message from the point of view of the other as well as our own.

Independently of meanings, swinging back and forth between the self and other viewpoint also has a great advantage in the realm of emotions. In this process, one is able to access otherwise occluded emotions. One can experience one's feelings from the point of view of the other, which may be less painful than feeling them as one's self. The state of balance, which I referred to in an earlier work (Scheff 1979) as "optimal distance," suggests how solidarity and love benefit close relationships whether in families or psychotherapy.

Mutual understanding often fails to occur, of course. Yet if a society is to survive it must occur more often than not. When we find that our friend with whom we made a dinner date shows up at the right time and place, we realize that he was not joking or lying. Driving an automobile safely requires taking the role of other drivers. In making a loan, a bank must usually accurately understand the intention of the customer to repay. In fact, our whole civilization is possible only to the extent that mutual understanding usually occurs.

It may help to understand this process by also considering contexts where mutual understanding breaks down. There is a debating tactic that is sometimes used in conversation such that one or both of the speakers doesn't actually hear the other person out. In the quarrel mode, this practice takes the form of interrupting the other person mid-sentence. But there is also a more subtle mode, where one party listens to only the beginning of the other's comments. Instead of continuing to listen until the other is finished, the "listener" instead begins to construct his own retort, based only on the first few sentences that the other has uttered. This practice is difficult to detect, and has probably never been studied empirically. But it represents one source for the breakdown of pendulation, and therefore of mutual understanding.

Certain types of personality also tend toward lack of mutual understanding. Narcissism, for example, is a tendency to see the world only from one's own viewpoint. This idea is played out in detail in the film *As Good as It Gets*. The character played by Jack Nicholson falls for the character played by Helen Hunt. But he has great difficulty in relating to her because he must struggle to get outside his own point of view. The last scene, in particular, portrays the agony he suffers in trying to take her point of view as well as his own.

There is also a personality type with the opposite difficulty, balancing one's own point of view against the others. Perhaps there is a passive or dependent personality type whose penchant is to stay in the other person's viewpoint, rather than balancing it against one's own. I have personally known professional actors and politicians who had no secure bond because they seemed not to have a point of view of their own. A relationship may be relatively stable when the personality styles of the two persons are opposite. A person with a narcissistic or isolated style might fit with a person with a dependent or engulfed style. The first person would expect the second to take his point of view, and the second person would expect the other person not to. But in *As Good as It Gets*, the Helen Hunt character would not put up with the male character's lack of empathy: she clearly showed that he would have to change his ways. Undoubtedly there are many other sources of lack of mutual understanding that require investigation.

In struggling to define what is meant by a sexual perversion, the philosopher Thomas Nagel (1979) came very near to defining normal, or at least non-perverse sex in terms of attunement.[2] Although he doesn't use that term, or any of the others I have used, such as intersubjectivity, his definition of non-perverse sex in terms of each knowing that the other knows they desire and are desired certainly implies it:

> These [sexual] reactions are perceived, and the perception of them is perceived; at each step the domination of the person by his body is reinforced, and the sexual partner becomes more possessible by physical contact, penetration, and envelopment. (48)

In another passage, he invokes the idea of unity and oneness. He goes on to propose that sex between two persons is perverse if it lacks this kind of self and mutual awareness. He points out that this definition inevitably broadens the definition of perversion; ordinarily one doesn't consider it perverse if one or both of the partners is imagining being with someone else other than the person with whom they are having sex. The idea of mutual awareness, with or without sexuality, is closely linked to a theory of social solidarity.

Solidarity and Alienation

In the framework proposed here, the non-genetic component of love would be one type of solidarity, a *secure bond* (Bowlby 1969), involving shared awareness between lovers. As Solomon has suggested, the love bond also means sharing of identity.

There are many passages in literature that imply the idea of shared identity between lovers. Here is an example from *Wuthering Heights*, in which Cathy, the heroine, exclaims that she IS her lover:

> I cannot express it; but surely you and everybody have a notion that there is or should be an existence of yours beyond you. What were the use of my creation, if I were entirely contained here? My great miseries in this world have been Heathcliff's miseries, and I watched and felt each from the beginning: my great thought in living is himself. If all else perished, and he remained, I should still continue to be; and if all else remained, and he were annihilated, the universe would turn to a mighty stranger: I should not seem a part of it.... Love for Heathcliff resembles the eternal rocks beneath: a source of little visible delight, but necessary. Nelly, I AM Heathcliff! He's always, always in my mind: not as a pleasure, any more than I am always a pleasure to myself, but as my own being.

However, the passage "He's always, always in my mind" suggests a lack of balance, at least on the heroine's part. Rather than loving

Heathcliff, from the point of view of the definition offered here, she seems to be engulfed by and obsessed with him.

The amount of sharing of identity is crucial for a secure bond. Each lover needs to treat the other as of equal value as self, *neither more nor less*. The idea of valuing self and other equally means that the loving person can see both persons' needs objectively, without overvaluing self or other. This idea is represented in the airline instructions that the parent place the oxygen mask on her/his face first, not on the dependent child.

The idea of love involving equality of self and other has been touched on by many earlier discussions. Sullivan (1945, 20) states the idea exactly: "When the satisfaction or the security of the other person becomes as significant to one as is one's own satisfaction or security, then the state of love exists." Note that he doesn't say that the other is *more* significant, only *as* significant. But like most of the other discussions of this point, Sullivan doesn't dwell upon it or provide examples. It is mentioned casually, and in passing.

This idea can be linked to the more general framework of social integration (alienation/solidarity). True love involves being neither dependent (engulfed) nor independent (isolated), but interdependent, to use Elias's terms (1972). It is particularly important to distinguish between a secure and an engulfed bond, since most social science confounds these two types.

In an engulfed bond, one or both partners give up basic aspects of self in order to be loyal to the other. In a traditional marriage, for example, the wife often suppressed anger and resentment to the point that it seemed to disappear, in order to be loyal to her husband. Perhaps this is the major source of emotional estrangement in long-term relationships.

Those who are infatuated or heartbroken with "love" do not have a secure bond. In cases of infatuation at a distance, the contact that is necessary for the development of attunement is missing; there goes "love at first sight"! Even where there is contact, the infatuated or heartbroken one may be self-absorbed (isolated) or engulfed to the point that attunement cannot occur. As indicated in the last chapter, these two states are often presented in popular song lyrics as if they were genuine love.

Solidarity and alienation are usually discussed as if they were macro phenomena, occurring only in large groups or even whole societies. But these concepts are also useful at the level of inter-personal relations, both over long spans of time and also moment by moment.

Love is usually thought of as long term, involving commitment to the relationship. But love can also be seen dynamically, by observing an ongoing dialogue. In fact, the moment by moment occurrence of love and other emotions may point toward an important issue in defining attunement in genuine love.

Marshall Rosenberg (1999), defining what he calls "non-violent communication," has suggested that in close relationships, maintaining empathic connectedness (attunement) must be treated as more important than any particular topic being discussed. This idea seems to go to the very heart of genuine love, since it brings up the issue of impediments to love and resulting lapses.

In Rosenberg's workshops, this question often arises in parent-child relationships, when a mother or father complains about a child's behavior. For example, a mother may repeat dialogue between her and her son about getting his homework done before watching TV or playing electronic games. Rosenberg begins by explaining that the child has a need for autonomy, for being his own person, as well as a need for remaining connected with the parent.

This idea seems to be lost on the parent. She or he will ask: "So how do I get him to do the homework?" The parent seems to have the idea that what is involved is a test of wills, and that the way to go is to have a stronger will than the child. Rosenberg then goes on to explain that the parent needs to show that empathic connectedness is more important to her than getting the homework done. That is, that she respects the child's need for autonomy.

In terms of love, Rosenberg's idea implies that in genuine love, the lovers show that maintaining attunement is usually more important than anything else. That is, *nothing outside of the relationship (work, children, household tasks, and so on) is more important than the relationship itself.*

One implication is that any kind of ultimatum, no matter how subtle, violates the love contract. One of the ways this issue comes up is in discussions of commitment between men and women. Because of differences in upbringing, often it is the woman in a relationship who confronts the man about his commitment. Typically, both sides behave badly in this confrontation. Here is a dialogue between students in one my classes that illustrates the problem.

Janey and Charley have been dating for two months, seeing each other every day. But one day Charley doesn't call or show up.

> JANEY phones: What's going on, Charley, are you still interested in me?
> CHARLEY: I don't know.
> JANEY: You don't know?
> CHARLEY: Well, I just need some time and space right now.

Confronted by Janey, Charley appears to feel cornered. It doesn't matter whether he actually doesn't know or if he is just stalling. He has disconnected. Whatever love the two have for each other is not happening in this particular episode, because there is no attunement.

Although lovers often confront each other with direct questions about degree of commitment, a more diplomatic approach would probably work to maintain the bond, or at least settle the issue more quickly and with less pain. For example, if Janey had opened the discussion by leaving off "are you still interested in me?" (What's going on Charley?), Charley may have entered into the dialogue instead of disconnecting from it. Rosenberg's idea of maintaining empathic connectedness (attunement) seems to have many implications for understanding the meaning of love, and love's maneuvers.

The idea of attunement also may help to understand the intensity of the feeling of love. Balanced attunement is a way of describing a secure bond; the corresponding emotion is genuine (authentic) pride. Just as shame and embarrassment are the emotions of lack of attunement, so pride is generated by attunement. Even for non-erotic love, the conjunction of feelings of attachment and genuine pride, and the absence of sadness and shame presumably can give rise to powerful sensations of well-being. In erotic love, when further conjoined with sexual arousal, these three different rivers of sensation may be one of the most intensely pleasurable experiences in all of life.

To understand the emotional components of love, it is necessary to consider both the presence and the absence of emotions. First consider the emotions connected with attachment and separation. Sadness (grief) is the crucial indicator of attachment: we miss the other when she or he is away, and we are struck down with grief at their loss. But what is the emotion connected with the presence of the other? Joy is too strong a word for this feeling. I suppose one might say that rather than feeling a particular feeling, one merely feels normal, or the absence of pain.

But the situation may be a bit more complex than it seems. Suppose that in modern industrial/urban societies, one experiences a sense of separation from others early on in childhood. There is such intense pressure for individuation and individual achievement and recognition that we are practically forced to separate ourselves from others. Not just our parents, but from all others, even, to some extent, from those closest to us.

Supposing, for the sake of discussion, that modern societies give rise to this kind of extreme separation in virtually everyone; what would be the consequences? There are two that I think are relevant to understanding the emotion of love. First, we all learn to defend against feelings of loneliness and isolation. That is to say, we learn to suppress and/or ignore these painful feelings. Second, however, this kind of maneuver is usually only partially successful. Most of us go through most of our life bearing at least a hint of sadness as background to our activities.

Genuine love silences this background noise, at least temporarily. When one is connected with the loved one(s), one feels normal in the sense of sadness being absent. Love can be the absence of sadness, as if a heavy weight has been lifted. One is no longer alone in the universe.

The same reasoning applies to the presence of pride that accompanies the shared identity and awareness during moments of genuine love. The feeling of authentic pride that is registered is not only that of the emotion itself, but also, and probably much more intensely, the absence of the background noise of humiliation, shame, and embarrassment.

Not only sadness, but shame and embarrassment, real or anticipated, are a continuing presence in the life of denizens of modern societies. Goffman's first and best known book, *Presentation of Self in Everyday Life* (1959), made this point in many different ways. His Everyperson is constantly aware of her or his standing in the eyes of the others, but helpless to do anything about it, and is usually anticipating, or often, actually experiencing shame or embarrassment. Perhaps the most powerful feelings connected with love concern not only the presence of pleasurable emotions, but the absence of painful ones. This chapter reviewed earlier conceptions of genuine love, showing the division of opinion and the lack of agreement on the meaning of love. The review of current approaches to love suggests a new definition, which will be further discussed in a later chapter.

Notes

1. I couldn't find this passage in any of Huxley's essays, and Bloom himself was unable to remember the citation.

2. Ronald de Sousa called this essay to my attention.

CHAPTER 3

EMOTION
LANGUAGES

*Love, Pride, Anger, Grief, Fear,
and Other Emotions*

It would appear that popular songs provide a confusing picture of emotions, especially love and the feeling of being rejected. These kinds of difficulties are not limited to popular songs, but occur equally in the larger society. Especially in the English language, the conventional names used for emotions turn out to be ambiguous, confusing, and in large measure, deceptive. In the spectrum of emotions, there may be no word for one color, too many words for another, and green can mean yellow and purple. Our emotion lexicon seems to conceal more than it reveals.

This chapter will document the problem of emotion ideas in the English language and suggest a provisional way of overcoming it, new definitions of some of the basic emotions, and a theory of the social-emotional world. With this scheme we will be able to clarify the way in which popular love songs both reveal and conceal emotions.

People who live in modern societies have grown accustomed to thinking that their societies are advanced in every way, that progress is comprehensive and total. In the realms of technology and mastery of the outer world, there are certainly grounds for this belief. Yet there are some areas that are not advanced, or that may even be regressing. The realm of emotions seems to be one of these areas.

The meaning of the emotion names that are used in modern societies seem self-evident to the average person to the point that they are taken for granted. To propose, as this chapter will, that these meanings need to be changed may seem utterly without foundation, as if I were to propose that the sun revolves around the earth. Nevertheless, if we are to make sense of popular love songs and, to a large extent, our lives, this is the direction that needs to be taken.

The hiding of the emotional world in Western societies begins with the avoidance and disguise of feelings. There seem to be three main lines of defense against emotions:

1. Ignoring them. Most discussions, both in lay and expert language, don't mention emotions. Objects, behavior, thoughts, beliefs, attitudes, images, and perception are discussed, but not emotions. This is by far the most prevalent defense. Until recently the social sciences had no sections devoted specifically to the study of emotions. Even after such sections have been established, they remain small enclaves lost among vast numbers of other specialties.

2. When emotions are mentioned, as they are beginning to be, the references are usually at so abstract and general a level as to amount to dismissal. The word *emotion*, and terms like *feeling, hurt, anxiety, emotional arousal*, or *upset*,

refer to such a variety of states as to be almost useless. Just as the idea of "the rational man" in legal discourse leads to a dismissal of the vast domain of irrationality, so the use of highly abstract and general emotion terms negates the realm of emotions.

3. The final line of defense is that even words that seemingly refer to specific emotions are wildly ambiguous and/or mask one emotion with another. Most of this chapter will be devoted to briefly outlining some of these usages, with specific reference to fear/anxiety, anger, pride, shame, embarrassment, grief/sadness, and love. The comments on shame and love below are preliminary to full treatments of these emotions in later chapters.

The realm of emotions in the West is beset by an elemental difficulty: the meanings of words that refer to emotion are so ambiguous that we hardly know what we are talking about. Virginia Woolf said it succinctly: "The streets of London have their map; but our passions are uncharted" (*Jacob's Room*). Compared to maps of the material world, and the social science of behavior, thoughts, attitudes, perception, and beliefs, the realm of emotions is *terra incognita*.

Both laypeople and experts disagree on almost everything about emotions. For example, several studies have pointed out the lack of agreement on which emotions are basic. Ortony et al. (1988, 27) show no agreement on this issue among twelve investigators, some leading experts in the field. Even the number of such emotions, much less the specific emotions, is in contention; the fewest proposed is two, the most, eleven. There is not a single emotion word that shows up on all 12 lists. Plutchik (2003) also shows complete disagreement (see the table of 16 theorists on p. 73).

This disagreement involves emotion words in only one language, English. The comparison of emotion words in different languages opens up a second chaos. Anthropological and linguistic studies suggest that just as the experts disagree on the number and names of the basic emotions, so do languages. Cultural differences in emotion words will be mentioned here, but it is such a major issue that brevity forbids the attention it requires.

There are by now many studies that compare either emotion words or still photos of facial expressions in different languages/cultures, finding mostly similarities. The problem with these studies is that in order to use a quantitative ("scientific") format, they have focused entirely on the words or still photos themselves, omitting nonverbal and/or contextual elements. But the meaning of emotion words, particularly, is largely dependent on these extraverbal components. The phrase "I love you" can mean everything or nothing, depending on how it is said and in what context. Leaving out either nonverbal components (as in Shaver 1992) or contextual ones (as in the still photo studies of facial expressions) invalidates the findings.

In their study of limbic communication, Lewis et al. (2000) make a similar observation with respect to formulaic approaches to psychotherapy (184). Applying their idea to the present topic, comparisons of languages that ignore nonverbal and/or contextual components of emotion words will find them "like Reader's Digests condensed books—where, by purging the particular, the stories are strangely identical."

The supply of emotion words in the West, particularly in English, is relatively small. Although English has by far the largest total number of words (some 600,000 and still expanding), its emotion lexicon is smaller than other languages, even small languages like Maori. In addition to having a larger emotion lexicon than English,

Maori emotion words are relatively unambiguous and detailed compared to English (Metge 1986). As indicated above, in Western societies, emotions are seldom even mentioned. Or if mentioned, only abstractly, avoiding specifics. The last stage of defense is that even when specific emotions are mentioned, usage of these words helps to confirm the emotional status quo. Some examples follow.

Pride

This word has two distinct meanings in current usage, one positive, the other negative. The dominant one is negative, as in the Biblical "Pride goeth before a fall." This usage confounds the positive meaning, authentic or justified pride, with arrogance, egotism, or self-centeredness. It is quite possible that negative "pride" might be the opposite of genuine pride, a defense against shame. In order to convey appreciation of pride, it must be modified by an adjective. The word pride alone, the default position in English, is negative. Even if one adds a supportive adjective, like genuine or justified, the word is still tainted.

Fear/Anxiety

Before Freud, fear meant the emotional signal of physical danger to life or limb, and anxiety was a lesser fear. But after Freud, anxiety became broad enough to include any kind of diffuse or unclear emotion. Current vernacular usage is so enlarged that fear can be used to mask other emotions, especially shame and humiliation. "I fear rejection" has nothing to do with danger of bodily harm. It refers rather to the anticipation of shame or humiliation. (When I first explain this nicety to students, their eyes glaze over.) *Anxiety* has become an abstract, pliable word like *emotion* or *arousal.*

Love

In current usage, *love* is so broad as to include almost any kind of positive feeling, including extremely dysfunctional ones. The title of the mass market hit *Women Who Love Too Much* illustrates this usage. Women who are so pathologically passive and dependent as to allow their husbands to abuse them and/or their children explain that they don't leave because they love their husbands too much. *Love,* a positive word, is used to deny and conceal an alienated relationship that is explosively destructive. Yes, this usage is perfectly proper in English.

Current usage also confounds genuine love, which surely means loving someone that we know, warts and all, with infatuation, which deletes warts and any other blemish. Infatuation is an idealized fantasy of another person, often based on appearance alone. In this way, the word *love* is used to hide a failure to connect with a real person, i.e, alienation.

Grief/Sadness/Distress

There is a collective misunderstanding in Western societies about the nature of grief, the emotion of loss. Even in societies that maintain collective rituals of mourning, grieving the loss of a close attachment is apt to be lengthy and consuming. But in Western societies the person in mourning is usually given little time. After a few weeks, expressions of grief are not encouraged, if not actively condemned: "get a grip, take a pill, see a shrink." For most people in modern societies it is almost impossible to understand that a long siege of grief and mourning is often natural and necessary.

Anger

The confusion over the meaning of this word seems to be different than any of the above problems. It involves confounding the feeling of anger with acting out anger, that is, confusing emotion and behavior. We don't confuse the feeling of fear with running away, the feeling of shame with hiding one's face, or the feeling of grief with crying. But anger is thought to be destructive, even though it is only a feeling, not an action.

The feeling of anger is an internal signal, like any other emotion. It is one of the many signals that alert us to the state of the world inside and around us. In itself, if it is not acted out, it is instructive, not destructive.

When anger is expressed in verbal form, rather than acted out as screaming or aggression, it can be constructive: "I am angry because … " It explains to self and other where one is, how one is frustrated, and why. Both self and other need to know this information. The confounding of anger expression with acting out can be seen as a way of justifying acting out, rather than expressing anger, and therefore the prevalence of acting out, as in spousal abuse and road rage. Like the other confounds, this one attempts to justify and conceal the profound alienation between persons when anger is acted out rather than expressed verbally. The former both reflects and generates disconnection; the latter can lead to connection. "Things aren't right in this relationship because.... "

Shame

In contrast to the nearly limitless pliability of the word *love*, current usage of *shame* in English usually involves only one meaning, an extremely narrow one: a crisis feeling of intense disgrace. In this usage, a clear distinction is made between embarrassment and shame. Embarrassment can happen to anyone, but shame is conceived as horrible. Embarrassment is speakable, shame is unspeakable. This usage avoids everyday shame such as embarrassment and modesty, and in this way sweeps most shame episodes under the rug.

Other languages, even those in modern societies, treat embarrassment as a milder version of shame. In Spanish, for example, the same word (*vergüenza*) can be used to mean either. Most languages also have an everyday shame that is considered to belong to the shame/embarrassment family. For example, the French *honte*, disgrace shame, as against *pudeur*, which can be translated as modesty, or better yet, a *sense of shame*. If you ask an English speaker if shame is distinct from embarrassment, they will answer with an impassioned "yes." A French speaker might ask, "Which kind of shame?"

Comments by several native speakers of German suggest to me that their language is moving toward the English language model of denying everyday shame. They say that in contemporary German, since the word for disgrace shame (*schande*) is seen as old fashioned, the word for everyday shame (*scham*) is being used in its place. This usage is probably making shame less speakable, as in the English language model. A similar phenomenon may be happening with pride. The negative version (*hochmut*) is now seen as old fashioned, so that the positive version (*stolz*) may be confounding a positive feeling with a negative one. I suspect that what current German speakers mean by old fashioned is that *schande* and *hochmut* were staples in Hitler's usage, so are no longer viable. I would like to get more votes on this issue from German speakers, since my own knowledge of modern German is dated.

It seems to me that the language used by emotion experts is no clearer than that used by laypersons. Emotion researchers use a wide variety of emotion names: there are many different names used for what seems to be the same emotion, each seemingly connoting a subtle or sometimes a flagrantly different meaning.

One example would be the emotion that is usually called grief in the clinical literature, that follows from loss of an attachment or anticipation of that loss. There is a very large literature on attachment and on child development that uses the term *distress* instead of grief. Distress is much broader than grief since it connotes physical as well as emotional pain, and implies consciousness more than grief.

Silvan Tomkins (1962) seems to have started the use of the word *distress* rather than *grief*. In the first three volumes of *Affect/ Imagery/Consciousness* (1962, 1963, 1965) the word *distress* is used frequently, with the word *grief* occurring only on one page (V.2, p. 6). However, in Volume IV (1992), there is an abrupt change: distress disappears, its place apparently taken by grief.

In the first three volumes it is fairly clear what Tomkins means by distress, because he connects distress to loss and crying. In Volume IV, he makes this connection using only the word *grief*. What happened? As far as I know, there has been no published response to this dramatic change in nomenclature.

The original studies of facial expression of emotion followed Tompkins's first usage: neither Ekman and his colleagues nor Izard refer to grief. However, later works, such as Harre and Parrott, refer only to grief, never to distress. Plutchik (2003) also refers only to grief. Others use the word *sadness*, rather than *distress* or *grief*. Volkan (1988, 1997, 2004), one of the leading theorists of conflict, uses an entirely different nomenclature. What I would call *unresolved grief*, a standard diagnostic category in psychiatry, plays a central role in his work. Yet instead of referring to it, he uses only the phrase "the failure to mourn." This usage behaviorizes, and therefore disguises an emotion.

I have found only one explicit discussion of the relationship between distress and grief, in Izard (1977). What he proposed, that distress is the primary affect of which grief is only one ingredient, seems to me the exact opposite of the majority understanding: grief is the primary affect. However, in a recent publication (2004), it is clear that Izard has, like Tomkins, switched terminology. He doesn't switch from distress to grief, as Tomkins did in his 1992 volume, but from distress to sadness. As with Tomkins, there is no explanation of the change.

There are many other emotion words run amok in studies and discussions of emotion. The broad usage of *fear* and *anxiety*, referred to above, is one instance. There have been several surveys of the occurrence of specific emotions in large groups, but the results are ambiguous. For example, when a subject is asked about his or her anger events, a detailed definition of anger that is inclusive of the cognate emotion words the subjects might use is not offered by the researcher. Without such a definition, however, it is not clear whether the distribution in the group studied that results refers to emotions or to *the emotion words* that are current. I have noticed, for example, that my students often use the term "pissed off" rather than angry, and surprisingly, that some of them do not connect this feeling with anger. These latter students, if asked about their anger events, might reply that they don't have them.

Aaron Lazare told me about a similar experience he had in an actual anger study he did. At one point he was meeting with groups of elderly Jewish women in NYC to investigate their experiences of emotion. When he came to anger, however, each group denied its occurrence. He tried many cognates (irritated, annoyed, etc.), but there was silence until he mentioned "aggravation." Everyone responded enthusiastically with raised hands and murmurs of recognition. In one group a woman cried out: "Oy gewalt! Have we got aggravation!"

In studies in English in which emotions go undefined, there are likely to be different understandings by researchers, the subject, and readers. We need concepts of emotions so that these different groups will understand each other within and between the three groups.

Discussion

All of these confusions and limitations help maintain the status quo in the realm of emotions: individualism and the subordination of feeling to thought and behavior. The broad use of the word *love* and the narrow meaning of the word *shame* may be central to this end.

Referring to all kinds of slightly positive or even negative relationships with the positive word love helps disguise the miasma of alienation and disconnection in modern societies. Similarly, defining shame narrowly, as only disgrace shame, helps mask disconnection. Since this latter idea is not obvious, it will be necessary to discuss it further.

Suppose that just as fear signals danger of bodily harm, and grief signals loss, shame signals disconnection. In modern societies, since connecting with others seems to be infrequent, we hide that fact. Instead of saying that we were embarrassed, we say "It was an awkward moment for me" or some such. This particular usage involves a complex maneuver: it was the *moment* that was awkward (projection), not me that was embarrassed (denial). We writhe and churn to avoid contact with our emotions, even contact that is merely verbal.

In English especially, there is a vast supply of words that can be used as alternatives to the word *shame*. Retzinger (1995) lists more than a hundred vernacular codewords that can be used to refer to shame without using the s-word, under six headings:

> *Alienated:* rejected, dumped, deserted, etc.
> *Confused:* blank, empty, hollow, etc.
> *Ridiculous:* foolish, silly, funny, etc.
> *Inadequate:* powerless, weak, insecure,
>   unworthy, inadequate, etc.
> *Uncomfortable:* restless, tense, anxious, etc.
> *Hurt:* offended, upset, wounded, etc.

The use of rejected ("I feel rejected") and rejection ("I fear rejection") is particularly prevalent. The name for a behavior (rejecting) that causes shame is used to disguise the underlying emotion.

The broadening use of *fear* and *anxiety* seems to be another way of disguising shame. To say that one fears rejection, or to use a term like social anxiety or social fear, is to mask the occurrence of shame and embarrassment. The many variants of dignity and indignity can serve a similar function.

We can also disguise the shameful pain of rejection by masking it with anger or withdrawal and silence. Similarly, the negative version of pride can be used to mask a defense against shame as too much pride. Studies of stigma and of indignities, even though these words signify shame, seldom take note of the underlying emotion, concentrating instead on thoughts and behavior.

Apologies suggest another instance of the masking of shame with another emotion. The ritual formula for an apology in the English language is to say that you are *sorry*. The word sorry (grief) serves to mask the more crucial emotion of shame. "I'm ashamed of what I did" is a much more potent apology than the conventional "I'm sorry" (Scheff 1994; Miller 1993).

This chart will allow us to navigate the language of love in popular songs.

Table 3.1 Chart of Emotion Names

Name	Source	Signs
Grief	Loss	Sadness, crying
Fear	Physical Danger	Alarm, shaking, and sweating
Anger	Frustration	Intense focus, rapidity of thought and speech
Pride	Attunement (connectedness)	Satisfaction
Shame	Disconnection	Feeling unworthy, alone
Family Love	Attunement and attachment	Miss the person when he/she is away
Romantic love	Attunement, attachment, and sexual attraction	

The hiding of emotion is connected with gender differences in the management of emotion. Until quite recently, males were being routinely socialized for achievement in the outer world, women for dealing with the inner world of home and family. This difference was closely connected to industrialization and urbanization: men were usually in the forefront of this change, rather than women. In any event, the result is that as men became more dominant over women, the suppression of emotions was reinforced by their domination.

The banishment of emotions from discourse and thought in modern societies both reflects and generates alienation. One way of countering this trend would be to *acknowledge* emotions, rather than denying them. Rediscovery of the emotion world may be a crucial step in helping us to understand ourselves and our society.

In order to discuss the emotion language in popular songs, we need a spectrum of emotion words different from those that are routinely used in our society. In the absence of agreement among the experts, I will use my own tentative spectrum in order to understand popular love songs, as it is implied above. Note that in this chart the meaning of love is greatly narrowed compared to the vernacular meanings, and the meaning of shame is greatly expanded.

The process of industrialization and urbanization has been influencing spoken English longer than any other language, since industrialization began in England. In this chapter I propose that modernization has led to the downplaying of emotions and relationships in spoken English to a greater degree than in any other language, in favor of emphasis on thought, behavior, and individualism. As this process continues, the social-emotional world seems to be vanishing from awareness in English-speaking countries, and to a somewhat lesser degree, in other Western societies.

Two Key Dimensions of the Social-Emotional World

Having sorted through some of the problems of emotion terminology, we are now prepared to deal with a theory that links emotions and social relationships. The approach to understanding human emotions and relationships in this book involves two fundamental ideas. With respect to emotions, this idea is framed in terms of degree of distance or involvement. The second idea concerns relationships, the degree of connectedness. As will be noted below, these two ideas are closely related. The idea of distance from emotions will be discussed first.

Drama theory has long held that the degree of emotional distance between audience and the characters is the key feature of all drama. In an earlier book (1979) I further proposed that aesthetic (optimal) distance involves a balance in the audience's perspective, being equally involved and detached from the drama.

When an audience is at optimal distance from the emotions evoked by the drama, it is both highly involved emotionally but also detached, continually knowing that it is only a drama. This distance allows members of the audience to feel their own emotions freely and with little pain, even grief, fear, and shame. With too much involvement, however, persons merely replay the painful part of these emotions. With too little involvement, there are no feelings at all. Without emotions, dramas evoke thoughts but not feelings, and are usually therefore dull or boring.

At optimal distance, one moves rapidly back and forth between involvement and detachment. This movement is usually so rapid that we are not aware of it. We experience feeling and thought in a way that feels as if the two modes were occurring simultaneously. As mentioned above, this rapid movement has been named *pendulation* (Levine 1997).

The idea of optimal distance also provides the basis for a way of considering relationships. The distancing of emotions discussed above involves internal pendulation, between feeling and emotion and observing ourselves feeling. Yet pendulation also can occur between persons. As discussed in Chapter 6, genuine love involves both unity and separateness between lovers, an optimal distance between them that can be called *attunement*. The movement back and forth between self and other occurs not only in genuine love, but in any social relationship. When this kind of relationship occurs between groups, it is called *solidarity*. The members of each group have a deep understanding with the members of the other group, if only temporarily.

Understanding spoken language requires social pendulation, because vernacular language usage is so fragmented, incomplete, and situational. Most words and phrases have so many possible meanings that we need to take the point of view of the speaker in order to know which of the meanings are being employed. People learn pendulation so early in childhood, and use it so well, they don't realize they are doing it. As mentioned earlier, Cooley (1922) wrote that "we live in the minds of others *without knowing it.*"

This chapter has introduced a theory of the close linkage between emotions and social relationships. It will be used below to help understand the ways emotions and relationships are represented in popular songs, and how these ways might be changed in future lyrics.

CHAPTER 4

ALIENATION IN TOP 40 SONGS 1930–2000

This chapter reports my study of Top 40 songs over a period of 70 years. The first step was to examine lyrics for recurring patterns. Romance songs come in a variety of forms.[1] I begin this study by proposing three major types: a *love* lyric involves reciprocated attraction and fulfillment. As it turns out, this type is only a small minority. The large majority involves unreciprocated attraction. I call *heartbreak* those that involve attraction to a lost love, and *infatuation* those that involve attraction to someone desired but who has not reciprocated. Finally, there is a *miscellany* of romance lyrics that are not classifiable as one of these three types. Almost all of these different types, even the love lyrics, contain hints of alienation and unresolved emotions.

Using Lyrics World on the Internet, I first surveyed the titles of popular lyrics in the United States. It contained all of the titles of the Top 40 for the years 1930–1999,[2] some 12,500. But not every title was accompanied by the corresponding lyric. About 9 percent of the lyrics for the titles listed were not available.

For a preliminary impression of the place of romance lyrics in the Top 40, I used statistical software (SAS) to count the occurrence of romance words in the titles. To detect changes during the seventy years, I divided the titles into three groups: 1930–1949 (3,594), which I will refer to as **1930 ...**) 1950–1979 (5,385) (**1950 ...**), and 1980–1999 (3,521) (**1980 ...**). As it turns out, the changes in proportions of the three types of lyric were very slight.

The most significant word for romance lyrics was *love*. It occurred 276 times during the first period, which is 7.6 percent of the titles, 490 times (9.1 percent) for the second period, and 365 times (10.4 percent) for the latest period. Another word associated with romance is *baby*. It is always used as a term of familiar address, rather than referring to an infant. It occurred 60 times (1.7 percent) in the first period, 149 (2.8 percent) in the second, and 36 (.67 percent) in the last.

As an indicator of what I will call heartbreak lyrics, I combined the counts of a group of words: *heartbreak, heartache, crying, tears, lonely, hurt,* and *pain*. The combined count for this group of words was 60 (1.7 percent) for 1930 ... , 122 (2.2 percent) for 1950 ... , and 81 (2.3 percent) for 1980....

Finally, as an indicator of what I will be calling infatuation lyrics, I used the words *crazy, mad, madly, madness, fall,* and *falling* (as in *falling in love*). (The words infatuation and crush are seldom used in titles: I counted only three instances during the entire 70-year period.) The combined count for this group of words was 32 (.90 percent) for the first period, 71 (1.2 percent) for the second, and 36 (1.0 percent) for the third.

These figures show a slight increase in the use of the word *love* and the heartbreak words in titles, and a slight variation in the use of *baby* and infatuation words. Perhaps a more significant implication is the stability in the use of these words over the three periods. The word counts suggest that types of popular romance songs may have the characteristic stability of collective representations.

One obvious problem in using counts of title words is that most romance lyrics do not contain the word *love* or any of the other indicator words in their titles. Indeed, many romance songs do not even contain them in their lyrics, e.g. "You've Really Got a Hold on Me"; "Got to Get You into My Life." Both of these lyrics concern romance of a particular *kind*, infatuation, but do not use any of the indicator words. In order to survey patterns of love lyrics and indicators of alienation in them, it was necessary to analyze them in the context of the entire song.

As already indicated, about 9 percent of the lyrics were not available on the Web site. The size of the lyric base that must be read is further reduced because of multiple entries of titles. Some of the most popular songs made the Top 40 several times, as sung by different artists. Duplication reduces the number of titles to be read to about 9,000 over the seventy years.

Because of the large number of lyrics available, I took a one-year sample of the Top 40 for each of seven decades,[3] with the years chosen at random. In my sample overall I read 776 lyrics. The bulk of the lyrics (408) were from the period 1970–1999. As will be indicated below, these lyrics were not only more numerous but also much more diverse and somewhat more difficult to classify than those of the earlier period.

Even so, I was able to divide the lyrics for all the sample years I read into five categories: *Not-romance, heartbreak, infatuation, love,* and *miscellaneous romance*. The results of my analysis are shown in the table below.

Table 4.1 Types of Songs, 1930–1999

	1930–1959	1960s	1970–1999	Total
Not Romance	26 25%	66 25%	111 27%	203 26%
Heartbreak	23 22%	76 29%	103 25%	202 26%
Infatuation	20 19%	50 19%	60 15%	130 17%
Love	16 16%	43 16%	44 11%	103 13%
Misc. Romance	18 17%	25 15%	90 22%	133 17%
	103 99%	260 99%	408 100%	771 99%

My classification of romance songs seems to be roughly in agreement with two earlier surveys. Christenson and Roberts (1998, p. 121) classified Top 40 songs 1980–1990, reporting that 73 percent of the 240 lyrics they examined concerned love relationships. Edwards (1994) surveyed the Top 20 for 1980–89, finding 72 percent of the 200 lyrics she analyzed refer to romantic or sexual relationships. Their figures, 73 and 72 percent, are quite close to the 73 percent that I found for romance songs in the closest comparable period in my analysis of the three sample years during 1970–1999.

The proportion of *love* songs decreased slightly in the period 1970–1999 (21 percent) compared to the proportion in the period 1930–1959 (27 percent). The proportion of *heartbreak* songs increased slightly in the later period, from 22 percent to 25 percent, and the proportion of *infatuation* songs decreased, from 16 percent to 11 percent. Perhaps the most significant pattern is the stability of the lyric patterns over the 70-year period. The majority of romance songs (heartbreak and infatuation) suggest alienation over the entire period, as I will propose below. Since there were many changes in the content of popular songs that occurred in this period, I will return to the issue of change below.

Infatuation, Love, and Heartbreak

What can be learned by an inspection of romance lyrics? The direction I have taken was to note recurring patterns in the lyrics, especially those related to the I–We balance. (For the elaboration that follows, I did not limit my search to the Top 40 sample years, but called upon all lyrics from the entire 70 years.)

The dictionary definition of infatuation, unlike the many definitions of love, is simple and straightforward: an unreasonable or foolish attraction to another person ("a strong but not usually lasting feeling of love or attraction for someone," Cambridge International Dictionary). However, my reading of the romance lyrics suggests that word is somewhat ambiguous. This ambiguity can be seen in the idea of "love at first sight," a frequent topic in popular songs.

Love at first sight means that one can "fall in love" upon seeing the loved one, usually without any other form of communication. For example, "Love Walked In" (1938):

> One magic moment and my heart seemed to know
> That love said hello though not a word was spoken.

A similar idea is expressed in many romance lyrics, often very crudely, as in "Just One Look" (1963):

> Just one look, that's all it took ...
> ...
> Til I can make you mine ...

Several Beatles songs involve love at first sight, as in "I Saw Her Standing There" (1964): The beginning of this verse describes the speaker's reaction upon seeing this girl. She is described as "beyond compare." Thusly, the speaker pursues a dance with the girl, although all the speaker knows is that she is seventeen and he finds her physically attractive.

> So how could I dance with another
> When I saw her standing there.

The central idea in all love-at-first-sight lyrics is that a single glance was all that was needed; falling in love is instantaneous and based completely on the appearance of the beloved. A second theme of many of these lyrics is that the beloved is a coming into reality of an idealized image held long before she or he appeared, as in "Long Ago and Far Away" (1944):

> Just one look and then I knew
> That all I longed for long ago was you.

And also:

> Dearly beloved, how clearly I see,
> Somewhere in Heaven you were fashioned
> for me ("Dearly Beloved" 1942)

The correspondence, or lack of it, between inner feelings and outer reality is an important issue in romance lyrics. Often the adored one fails to live up to the inner image, or even more frequently, fails to reciprocate sufficiently to enable the lover to know if she or he lives up to it.

> I've been near you, but you never notice me
> ...
> How I wish you were mine ("My Cherie Amour" 1969)

Most love-at-first-sight lyrics don't disclose the outcome. Those that do involve unreciprocated attraction, what I have been calling infatuation. But in real life, as contrasted with songs, love at first sight may also lead to reciprocated attraction; it is sometimes an accurate, if intuitive, understanding of the loved one. The dictionary definition doesn't allow for this case, but scholars have noted it. The most insistent is Persons (1988), who urges the idea that infatuation (she uses the word "crush") is a foretelling and a rehearsal of love.

Persons's point is important in understanding infatuation, if at the same time one concedes, as she doesn't, that some infatuations are not an accurate foretelling of love at all. Rather than leading to love, these other infatuations simply persist as desire at a distance, either with one adored person, or a succession of them. For this reason, we need to distinguish between two types of infatuation, the intuitive kind, based on an accurate, even if instantaneous understanding of the loved one, and another, and probably more frequent kind that entails little or no understanding of the adored person. Tennov (1979) probably decided to use the term *limerance* to include both love and infatuation because of this ambiguity.

To clarify the distinction between the two types, it will be necessary to examine some infatuation lyrics in detail. What are their chief characteristics? In my reading of *heartbreak* lyrics, it was clear that they involved pain and suffering. That is, they express the pain of loss.

Pain is not the main feature of infatuation lyrics, although it is expressed in some of them, the suffering of unrequited love. The chief feature is not pain, but impairment. Yet the dominant feeling of infatuation is positive. The idea of infatuation as a pleasurable experience in spite of impairment is expressed in "All Shook Up" (Elvis Presley 1957):

Well, please don't ask me what's on my mind
I'm a little mixed up, but I'm feeling fine.

These lines represent a key aspect of infatuation. Even though many infatuation lyrics state or imply mental confusion or other impairments, as this one does, this state is often experienced as pleasurable (the lover is "a little mixed up, but ... feeling fine."). Mental confusion, as in this instance, and other kinds of impairment occur in virtually all infatuation lyrics.

The idea of mental impairment is often expressed with a vivid imagery of mental disorder, of being crazy or insane. Many songs virtually equate love with mental disorder:

> I'm losin' my mind, girl
> 'Cause I'm goin' crazy. ("Crazy" 1994)
> Hey, I'm a lovesick son
> I'm crazy about her. ("Crazy About Her" 1989)
> It [love] surrounds me
> Over me like a sea of madness
> ("I Think I'm in Love" 1982)
> I want you to want me.
> I need you so badly I can't think of anything but
> you—("Goin' Out of My Head" 1964)

Other examples are:

> "You're Driving Me out of My Mind" (1966)
> "Crazy for You" (1985)
> "Crazy in the Night" (1985)
> "Crazy Love" (1978)
> "Crazy on You" (1976)
> "Crazy" (1961)

The equation is so complete that some lyrics use craziness as a synonym for love without implying impairment of function ("Crazy 'Bout Ya Baby" 1954), which is also common in ordinary discourse. But the idea of craziness in most romantic lyrics literally implies impairment of function, to the point of mental disorder, since the songs describe actual symptoms.

Types of Impairment: Mental and Physical

Many lyrics suggest impairment without using the word *crazy* or one of its cognates: loss of control, delusion, obsession, compulsion, loss of judgment, and so on. In addition, many romance lyrics describe physical impairments, such as loss of appetite, sleep, etc.

Compulsion is the inability to control one's thoughts or behavior: feeling or actually being out of control. The song "You've Really Got a Hold on Me" (1962) illustrates loss of control:

> I don't like you but I love you.
> I want to leave you, don't want to stay here

The element of compulsive thinking is clear in "Daydreaming" (1998):

> I try to change my thoughts,
> You keep my mind occupied.

The line "You keep my mind occupied" introduces one of the most prominent impairments of thought in infatuation lyrics, obsessive thinking. This idea often takes an extreme form, that life is meaningless without the love object, as in "Without You" (1994):

> I can't live, if living is without you.
> I can't live, I can't give anymore.

The same idea is prominent in "I Just Want to Be Your Everything" (1977):

> Oh, if I stay here without you, darling, I will die.

Obsession also can take an extreme form as stalking the love object, as in "Every Breath You Take" (1983):

> Every breath you take and every move you make
> ...
> I'll be watching you.

In "Addicted to Love" (1986), the lovestruck singer complains about himself:

> One-track mind, you can't be saved
> Another young love is all you crave.

In the song "Daydreaming," mentioned above, the singer's compulsive thinking is an aspect of her obsession:

> All day long I think of you
> I can't even think of things to do.

The same theme is clear in "Sittin Up in My Room" (1994):

> Baby, baby, baby, baby
> Think about you all the time.

The classic romance song of obsession is "Night and Day" (1932):

> ... I think of you
> Day and night, night and day, why is it so

"Bobby's Girl" (1962) shows obsession and clouding of judgment:

> Each night I sit at home
> Hoping that he will phone

This lyric illustrates impairment to the point of living in an unreal world.

Physical Impairment

The theme of impairment of bodily function is another common ingredient of infatuation lyrics. This song is actually titled "Infatuation" (1985):

> Early in the morning, I can't sleep
> I can't work and I can't eat

"Addicted to Love" (already mentioned) has the same theme:

> You can't eat, you can't sleep
> Another kiss is all you need.

The complaint in "I Get Weak" (1988) is similar:

> Can't walk, can't talk, can't eat, can't sleep.

"Crazy About Her" (1989) involves a litany of suffering:

> Can't get a good night's sleep, ain't been to work in weeks ...
> Can't get her off my mind, I'm drinking too much wine.

The song "Have You Ever" (1999) also complains about loss of sleep. It also introduces another impairment, lack of articulate speech:

> Have you ever tried the words,
> But they don't come out right?

The same complaint occurs in "I Get Weak":

> My tongue is tied, it's crazy.

The song "All Shook Up" also contains this kind of impairment:

> My tongue gets tied when I try to speak ...

The inability to speak clearly is closely related to the inability to speak to the love object at all, as in "I've Told Every Little Star" (1932):

> I've told every little star
> Why haven't I told you?

Very often infatuation lyrics imply that there has been no contact between the lover and the adored one. One example is "Shake Your Bon-Bon" (1999):

> I'm a desperado underneath your window
> I see your silhouette. Are you my Juliet?

The issue of contact and communication is important in understanding romantic love, but requires some theoretical background. I will take up this issue below. The next song takes it as given that "love" involves pain and impairment:

> This can't be love because I feel so well
> No sobs, no sorrows, no sighs
> ("This Can't Be Love" 1940)

Just as the pain of loss is the defining characteristic of heartbreak lyrics, impairment of mental and physical functioning is the most prominent feature of infatuation lyrics. This pattern is relevant to the I–We balance (to be discussed in Chapter 6), since the impairment that is described involves only the lover, not the loved one. The second most prominent characteristic is being lost in one's own bubble, usually called isolation.

Seeing the Actual Person

In many of these lyrics, there is no speech between the lover and the love object because there has not been, and may never be, any contact: love at first sight, or at a distance. In some love songs, in contrast, it is clear that there is or has been intimate contact. "The Way You Look Tonight" (1936) provides an example:

I will feel a glow just thinking of you.
And the way you look tonight ...
With each word your tenderness grows,
tearing my fear apart ...

The idea of little or no contact in infatuation raises the possibility that most of what takes place is in the smitten one's head, not in the real world, and certainly not in the love object. This idea is not expressed directly in infatuation lyrics, but may be implied by the way in which they describe the other person.

Most infatuation lyrics are unrealistic in regard to the adored one. They speak abstractly, in the language of idealization and exaggeration. These lyrics go into great detail about the lover's feelings, but about the desired one, use only abstract generalizations that could be applied to many persons. The adored one is beautiful, good, virtuous, generous, etc., but concrete features that might make them unique are never mentioned. Some examples:

You're just too good to be true
You'd be like heaven to touch.
("Can't Take My Eyes Off You" 1967)

He's like an angel, too good to be true.
("Angel Baby" 1958)

I've told every little star

Just how sweet I think you are.
("I've Told Every Little Star" 1932)

Infatuation lyrics leave out particulars, as when they assert that the adored is better in some undisclosed way than all others:

And the way she looked
Was beyond compare ("I Saw Her Standing There" 1964)

However, in the case of some of the earlier lyrics, the descriptions are more detailed and concrete, and therefore exceptional. These songs focus on the other person, noticing particulars about the loved one that make that person unique:

Moonlight becomes you, it softens your hair.
You certainly know the right things to wear.
("Moonlight Becomes You" 1942)

The absence of precise details and the prominence of generalized images tends toward sentimentality or fatuousness. Here is an example of the latter ("I Will Follow Him" 1963):

There isn't an ocean too deep ...
A mountain so high it can keep me away ...

These and quite similar lines are repeated to the point that one may think that the record is broken.

To summarize: the second prominent feature of infatuation lyrics (and most other romantic lyrics as well) is that they describe the adored one only abstractly. The feelings treated in these songs virtually all belong to the lover; very few of the adored one's feelings are mentioned. These features imply that the infatuated one is inside his or her own bubble, hardly considering the person they think they love (as indicated below, this is also true of most heartbreak and love lyrics). These lyrics are individualistic in the isolated mode. Finally, they suggest a constricted view of the world.

Constricted vs. Expanded View

The viewpoint of the infatuated one in these lyrics is focused on the adored one, who is the be-all and end-all; nothing else matters. Most of these lyrics say or imply that the infatuated one's vision is narrowly constricted.

In some of the earlier romance lyrics, by contrast, the lover's viewpoint seems to be expanded. In this lyric, the lover's view of the world expands to include sounds that he or she hadn't noticed before:

> There were bells on the hills
> But I never heard them ringing
> ("Til There Was You" 1957)

In the next lyric, the lover's vision expands to include both the world of nature and the human world:

> I see skies of blue and clouds of white
> I see friends shaking hands saying how do you do
> ("What a Wonderful World" 1959)

In this last instance, the lover's vision expands to include all of humanity:

There's a smile on my face
For the whole human race
("Almost Like Being in Love" 1947)

The issues of expansion and contraction of vision will appear again in the last chapter in regard to recent lyrics that concern the lover/ love object united against the whole world. To summarize the features of typical infatuation songs: they involve impairment of both mental and physical functions, they speak the language of idealized abstractions, and they usually involve constriction of vision. My analysis suggests that all infatuation lyrics and almost all romance lyrics in the Top 40 are individualistic, implying alienation in the isolated mode.

Heartbreak

The lyrics of heartbreak and infatuation differ in two ways. (Musical differences will be discussed below). As already indicated, infatuation lyrics concern desire for someone that one has not been involved with, heartbreak with someone that one has lost. The second difference is that some infatuation songs describe the state as pleasurable, but heartbreak songs rarely do; they usually concern pain and suffering, particularly the pain of grief and loneliness. Crying and tears are common in these lyrics. Just as impairment is one of the chief features of infatuation, pain is the chief feature of heartbreak. These lyrics contain less physical impairment than infatuation lyrics, but they are long on mental impairment, particularly compulsion and obsession. Hints of suicidal ideation are also not rare.

It was a surprise to find that most heartbreak lyrics, like infatuation lyrics, suggest that the heartbroken one is also lost in his or her own bubble. Like infatuation language, heartbreak lyrics usually involve abstract generalities, rather than the particulars that provide an image of the other person, and almost entirely concern the heartbroken one's feelings, rather than those of the lost one. Also like infatuation songs, virtually all heartbreak lyrics imply a constriction of vision, a focus on the lost one.

Conceptually one might expect that some heartbreak lyrics would evoke a particular person who was lost, and the work of mourning. Like infatuation, there should be two types. First is a heartbreak of mourning which suggests the image of the lost one and/or implies an expansion, rather than a constriction of vision. I have found few heartbreak lyrics that have this quality (described below). All the others are even more stereotyped than the infatuation lyrics. For that reason, I will be brief in analyzing heartbreak lyrics.

Here are some excerpts:

> Thinking of you till it hurts ...
> I'm all out of love, I'm so lost without you ...
> ("All Out of Love" 1980)

Heartbreak lyrics usually concern the feelings of the heartbroken one alone, not those of the lost one. However, this lyric, unlike most, guesses that the lost one feels the same as the singer, "hurt, tormented, and torn apart."

In addition to the pain of loneliness and feeling lost, this lyric implies an idea very common in heartbreak lyrics, that the heartbroken one is nothing without the lost lover. This is an important issue in conceptualizing the social relationship implied in songs, to be discussed below. "Can't Let Go" (1992), repeats these themes, with an emphasis on compulsion and obsession:

> My world is gone ...
> But still you remain on my mind

The lyric of "End of the Road" (1992) repeats the tears and crying theme, even though this song is from the male point of view:

> Girl, each time I try I just break down and cry
> Oh, I'd rather be dead

"Lately" (1998), is also male, but also features crying:

> Baby I'm on my knees praying God help me please,
> bring my baby back, right back to me

"Let Me Let Go" (1999) is sung by a woman, and implies obsession:

> I can't go a day without your face
> Goin' through my mind

The lyric "My Favorite Mistake" (1998) is also sung by a woman. It is more distanced and ironic than most heartbreak lyrics, and wittier, but it retains the theme of compulsion:

> Well maybe nothing lasts forever,
> I don't need forever after, but it's your laughter won't let me go

The lyric "Nobody Knows" (1996) continues the same themes, but also has the theme that the pain of denial can be added to the pain of heartbreak:

> I pretended I'm glad you went away
> The pain is real even if nobody knows

Lyrics that involved curtailment of feeling were rare before 1960, but plentiful ever since. I could find only one such song before 1960:

> Crying on the inside, laughing on the outside.
> Cause I'm still in love with you ("Laughing on
> the Outside [Crying on the Inside]", 1945)

The abrupt appearance (in the sixties) and continued presence since of popular lyrics that imply curtailment of feeling will be the topic of the next chapter.

Two heartbreak lyrics from the thirties are different in kind from all of the above: The first is "These Foolish Things" (1936):

> A cigarette that bears a lipstick's traces
> An airline ticket to romantic places
> And still my heart has wings
> These foolish things remind me of you ...
> How strange, how sweet, to find you still
> These things are dear to me
> They seem to bring you near to me

The second lyric is still more unlike the typical heartbreak lyric ("They Can't Take That Away from Me" 1937):

They may take you from me, I'll miss your fond caress.

But though they take you from me, I'll still possess:
The way you wear your hat
The way you sip your tea
The memory of all that
No, no, they can't take that away from me

Both of these lyrics imply successful mourning and unalienated love. They will be discussed at length in the last chapter.

Another lyric of this type, "I Love How You Love Me" (1961):

I love how your eyes close whenever you kiss me

...

I love how your heart beats whenever I hold you

This lyric is somewhat exceptional for the period 1960–1999, since it particularizes the loved one and describes her thoughts and feelings as well as the lover's.

There are more recent romance songs that attempt to particularize the beloved, but the result is usually vague or narrow. The Beatles lyric "Something" (1969) provides an example:

Something in the way she moves
Attracts me like no other lover

The cues to the beloved lack concreteness. She does not come alive from them.

In more recent periods, a few lyrics involve a single concrete description, most often eye color. But this single brief reference seems insufficient to bring the beloved to life.

In my search of the lyrics from 1970 to 1999, I could find only one obvious exception to the trend I have described, "Lady in Red" (1986):

> I have never seen that dress you're wearing
> *Or the highlights in your hair that catch your eyes* ...

The beloved is described in one concrete way, in the style of the exceptional romance lyrics of 1930–1969. Another possible exception is the song "The Best Things in Life Are Free," which implies that love brings an expansion of vision, which charted in 1992. But this song is something of an anomaly for my purposes since it first charted in 1927. I would appreciate it if any reader could name another Top 40 romance song from the period 1970–1999 that is an exception.

Discussion

Romance songs can be divided into four types: heartbreak, infatuation, love, and other. This section will interpret the meaning of these types in terms of a theory of social integration. Western societies currently focus on individuals to the extent that our relationship vocabulary is impoverished, especially relationships involving mutual understanding. Traditional and Asian societies, on the other hand, emphasize relationships to the point that the lexicon for individuality is meager. Neither East nor West has a vocabulary that equally includes relationship and individual.[4]

Emerson, one of the prophets of Western individualism, promoted self-reliance as an antidote to blind conformity: "When my genius calls, I have no father and mother, no brothers or sisters." But in a traditional society, there is NOTHING more important than one's relationships. Freeing up the individual from her relational/ emotional world has been at the core of modernization. Since one's relationships and emotions don't show up on a résumé, they have been de-emphasized to the point of disappearance.

As already indicated in Chapter 2, the individual/relationship problem is reflected in a longstanding dispute among scholars. At one extreme is the problem of Other Minds. Discussion of this issue asks "can one ever really know the mind of another person?" and answers the question with a resounding "No!" From this perspective, each individual is fated to stand alone, isolated from others.

However, there is an older tradition of scholarship that answers the question affirmatively. Historians, phenomenologists, and social psychologists have suggested that not only can one know the mind of others, but that the development of intelligence, cooperation, and even the individual self depends on being able to enter other minds. G. H. Mead built his theory of society on the ability that humans have to "take the role (that is, the viewpoint) of the other."

Like Mead, the psychiatrist Stern (1977) has pointed out that infant learning is dependent on what he calls "attunement" between infant and caretaker. The proponents of the intersubjective view argue that humans spend most of their waking lives imagining the viewpoints of others, and that a society exists to the extent that their imaginations are accurate.

From this point of view, consciousness is partly subjective, but it is also partly *intersubjective*. Cooperation with others, even avoiding automobile collisions, depends in large part on accurately understanding the intentions of others. In intimate relationships, the issue of connectedness has an added dimension, not only the sharing of outlook, but also the sharing of feeling. Mutual

understanding of thoughts and feelings is a key element in love between two people (see Chapter 6). A widespread failure to accurately
imagine the minds of others hints at dysfunctional relationships.
A society in which such alienation occurs, one would think, is in
danger of falling apart.

Social Integration

In theories of social integration, alienation takes two forms: separation from others (isolation) or estrangement from self (engulfment
with others out of loyalty). The theoretical approach most useful
for this study is found in Elias's (Introduction, 1987) discussion of
the "I–self" (isolation), the "we–self" (engulfment), and the "I–we
balance" (solidarity). Elias proposed a three-part typology: inde-
pendence (too much social distance), interdependence (a balance
between self and other that allows for effective cooperation), and
dependence (too little social distance). In solidarity, one understands the viewpoint of the other, but does not sacrifice one's own
viewpoint to it.

The issue of solidarity/alienation was at the core of the foundations of the discipline of sociology. European social philosophers
were deeply concerned that in the breakup of rural communities and
the growth of cities, communities of closely connected persons were
being replaced by cities largely composed of isolated individuals.

Later, more sophisticated thinkers, like Durkheim in *Suicide*, expanded the dichotomy between solidarity and alienation
into three terms, as indicated in the comments on Elias above.
Durkheim's terminology was different, but the idea is very similar
to Elias's: groups in which relationships are either too close or too
distant cause suicide or other pathologies. Not stated implicitly

in Durkheim but implied, is that it is possible for groups to have relationships that are secure, neither too close nor too distant. The threefold continuum of social integration is stated or implied in many sociological and social psychological theories in addition to Elias's (reviewed in Chapter 4 of Scheff 1997).

Marx's analysis of social systems resulted in a shift of focus in sociological theory. His work proposed that the central dynamism of social change was power rather than social integration. His focus on class and class conflict was mostly concerned with sources and consequences of power. But Marx also retained the older interest in social integration, through his concern with alienation.

Marx proposed that persons in capitalist societies become alienated not only from the means of production, but from others and from self. That is, that capitalism reflects and generates disturbances in social relationships and in the self. In his review of empirical studies of alienation, Seeman (1975) found evidence of both kinds of alienation: alienation from others and from self. Seeman referred to the latter as "self-estrangement," which is comparable to my term *engulfment*. (In suffocatingly close relationships, one gives up important parts of one's self in order to be loyal to the other[s].)

Although Marx supplemented his theory of class and power with a theory of alienation, there is great disparity in his development of the two theories. The political/economic theory is lavishly elaborated. The bulk of his commentary on alienation takes place in his early work. Even there, as in later works, the formulation of theory of alienation is brief and casual. It is easy to understand why Marx's followers have also made it secondary to material interests.

Perhaps any analysis of social structure and process should contain both axes: power and integration, the two major dimensions of any society. In this chapter, I emphasize solidarity and alienation, because it is seldom studied, but acknowledging that power is equally important. The threefold continuum of social integration suggests a way of analyzing the individual/relationship balance in song lyrics: to what extent do they evoke thoughts and feelings of self and other equally, suggesting solidarity rather than alienation? An empirical approach to the issue of solidarity/alienation in modern societies is to analyze collective representations, such as rites of mass mourning, mass advertising, or popular songs.

This chapter has shown that there are stable patterns of popular romance songs. Samples during the last 30 years suggest alienation in the isolated mode, rather than solidarity. The samples were similar during the period 1930–1950, but there were a few lyrics during that period that vividly portrayed solidarity.

My analysis so far has shown that types of romance songs, and the relative proportion of each type, have been fairly stable over the past 70 years, with only slight changes in proportions. These findings need qualification and elaboration, however. First, the analysis to this point has concerned only lyrics, the words of popular songs, not the music. Beginning in the '60s, massive changes in musical forms took place.

The typical romance song of 1930–1960 was a ballad. The musical form of the ballad is slow, somewhat detached in tone, with fairly simple orchestration as accompaniment. There is more emphasis on the lyrics than on the musical accompaniment. Beginning in the '60s, however, rock and roll erupted. The tempo and strong emphasis on rhythm increased so greatly as to suggest urgency, even desperation. The effect of this change is most noticeable in infatuation songs.

A comparison illustrates the change. Classic infatuation songs like "Night and Day" and "Long Ago and Far Away" were ballads.

They suggest emotion, but emotion that is under control. There is balance between thinking and feeling. More recent infatuation songs, such as "Got to Get You into My Life" and "You've Really Got a Hold on Me," with fast tempo and crashing rock rhythms, suggest more intense and overt emotions. The balance has shifted to the point that feeling dominates thinking.

Furthermore, beginning in the '60s, a change in the relative weight of the verbal and non-verbal elements began. In the later period, the music is increasingly dominant. Songs became longer, but with more repetitions of lines, decreasing the weight of the lines. Musical form and orchestration became more complex, but the lyrics are simplified. These changes, like the increasing tempo and strong rhythm, increase emphasis on feeling.

The mode of delivery by singers of romance songs also changed in this direction. The sixties saw the beginning of artists who yelled or screamed, like Aretha Franklin, rather than singing in a form resembling speech. James Brown was not a screamer, but his cries of delight were non-verbal, dominating usually somewhat insubstantial lyrics. All of these changes taken together are in the direction of emphasizing feelings over talking and thinking.

Even the content of lyrics themselves has changed over the seventy-year period more significantly than is suggested by the small changes and fluctuations shown in the word counts and lyric analysis reported above. Among romance songs, there are now many more genres than there were in the earlier period, all of which I have classified as *other* in my analysis. There are now romance songs about quarrels and disputes; some of these songs involve three persons. Typically, a woman is complaining about the competition for a man by another woman.

A whole new genre is the overt proposition, many of them floridly sexual. Although there were sexual songs in the earlier period, sex was seldom mentioned explicitly. "I'm a Sixty Minute Man" (1951) was unusual for its time, coming close to clear sexual meaning:

> There'll be fifteen minutes of teasin',
> fifteen minutes of squeezin'
> And fifteen minutes of blowin' my top

"Let's Spend the Night Together" (1967) is a good example. The clearest reference to sex is still somewhat indirect:

> I'll satisfy your every need (every need)
> And I now know you will satisfy me …

Even a song that was clearly understood to be sexual, "(I Can't Get No) Satisfaction" (1965), was mostly innuendo. However, the last stanza was much more direct than the other sexual songs of its time:

> I'm tryin' to make some girl
> Who tells me baby better come back later next week …

By the '90s, many of the Top 40 songs were openly sexual. The flagrant use of the word *fuck* suggests that in these lyrics love has nothing to do with it.

Another significant change has been the loosening and over-lapping of the three types of romance songs. The heartbreak lyrics have the least loosening, love next, and infatuation, the most. There are still many clearly identifiable representatives of each type in the most recent periods, but others show fewer indicators, especially love and infatuation. Another change is a tendency toward overlap between the types—love lyrics that have some of the characteristics of heartbreak or infatuation, for example. Here is an example of a love lyric that has considerable overlap with heartbreak ("How Do I Live" 1997):

> If I had to live without you
> What kinda life would that be

This lyric is in the subjunctive mood. The singer's attraction is reciprocated, but he or she anticipates heartbreak.

A love lyric from the thirties stands in stark contrast; rather than anticipating pain, it anticipates pleasure ("The Way You Look Tonight" 1936)

> Some day, when I'm awfully low, when the world is cold,
> I will feel a glow just thinking of you.
> And the way you look tonight ...

Here the future is anticipated positively, thankful for the present moment, whatever may happen afterward. It is a stirring tribute to the loved one, without idealizing her or him, and without being self-absorbed. In the thirties and forties, there were a few romance lyrics that implied solidarity rather than alienation. I have not been able to find many comparable lyrics for the last 40 years. There are exceptional lyrics during this period, but they meet the four criteria only very weakly.[5]

The last chapter will discuss a current lyric that at first seems to be an exception to this trend, but on close inspection proves not to be: "Better in Time," by Leona Lewis (2007).

Of Top 40 romance lyrics, I rated 4 percent (4/103) from the sample years 1930—1960 as meeting at least one of the four exception criteria that suggest solidarity; for the sample years 1960—1999, 1 percent (8/668). There are also fewer lyrics that meet more than one exception criteria in the later period: 3 percent for 1930–1960, only 1 for 1969–1999 (.002 percent). The vividness of the images that make lyrics suggestive of solidarity accentuates the difference between the two periods. Most of the exceptions in the earlier period are vivid; most of those in the later period are narrow, bland, or vague.

Conclusion

This chapter has shown that over the last seventy years, most romance lyrics involve patterns that feature individual desire rather than love relationships. A theory of social integration suggests that such lyrics imply alienation rather than solidarity. In this framework, solidarity involves a secure bond, a relationship featuring attunement between the lovers, and expansion of vision that includes the larger world beyond the immediate relationship. Most romance lyrics, on the other hand, involve only one side of the relationship, the lover's, their excitement or pain, impairment, and constriction of vision. The finding of fewer instances of lyrics that imply a mutual love relationship in the last forty years than in 1930–1960 suggests that alienation is increasing in romance lyrics.

To what extent does this change in romance lyrics correspond to changes in actual relationships in our society? The fact that these patterns have been relatively stable over many years may mean only that the songs that contain them have market appeal. It doesn't guarantee correspondence with social reality (Frith 1996).

It is conceivable that the patterns I have described are merely songwriting conventions. We cannot assume that mass appeal of heartbreak, infatuation, and love forms means that the audience is recognizing its own relationships in them. For example, the slight tendency in recent years to combine elements from the three genres, noted above, may be market driven. If a song can appeal to two of the three genres as a crossover, it could increase the size of the group that recognizes the form of the lyric, and therefore its market appeal. I believe that market forces explain the formation of these lyric genres, but only in part.

One market consideration likely to have considerable effect on the changes found in this study cannot be ignored: the increase in the youth market. The majority of the consumers in the earlier period were probably adults, but the majority in the later period were undoubtedly youths. This change might explain some of the simplification of romance lyrics reported here. Flagrant images of infatuation and heartbreak are more dramatic and easier for a ten-year-old to understand than mutuality, an idea not easily understood in Western societies, even by adults.

The theory of social integration outlined above provides an unexpected insight into the structure of romance songs. The narrowing of vision to the point of obsessing only about the beloved in the majority of romance lyrics suggests a dynamic frequently found in Western societies. The isolated person yearns for union (engulfment) with the other(s), the dynamic that seems to drive adherence to sects, cults, religions, and nations. In romance songs, the isolated lover, yearning for the beloved not yet attained, or lost, voices this desire. This yearning is part of a cruel trap, because it seems to suggest movement and growth, but may result only in a new form of alienation.

The most telling evidence of increasing alienation in this study is not found in the word counts and in the sampling of lyrics, the systematic techniques I used for this purpose giving, at best, only partial renderings of the contextual meaning of lyrics. The evidence that seems difficult to discount is that the lyrics that strongly imply security and solidarity in romantic bonds all come from the period 1930–1960. The indications of attunement, widening of vision, and enhancement of life are virtually absent in the sixties and after. Most of the romance lyrics since then imply lack of attunement, constriction of vision, or impairment of function—images of solipsistic self-absorption. The acceptance of such forms as romantic by songwriters, scholars, and the mass public hints at widespread alienation in our society.

The scholarly literature on love in the West is particularly surprising in this respect. The conception of love expressed there is every bit as individualistic as popular romance songs. This subject is too broad to be covered here, since there is a vast literature, both classic and modern, on the meaning of love. Instead, it will be the topic of the next chapter.

To make the point once again, the main findings reported here suggest alienation only in the lyrics, not necessarily in the larger society. These findings only add a further indication, like the increasing divorce and crime rates, and decreasing rates of civic engagement, that can be plausibly interpreted as increasing alienation.

To phrase it slightly differently, the findings in the study reported here suggest that the most popular romance lyrics seldom represent genuine love, but rather hidden forms of alienation.

Notes

1. For a descriptive study of romance songs as stages of courtship, see Horton 1957.

2. The count of titles for each year after 1950 is far greater than 40. The lists for 1950–1999 include titles on the Top 40 for even a single week during the year, which can lead to as many as two hundred and sixty one (1963) titles for each year. The years 1930–1949 deal only with the top 10 for each week, so that the total for these two decades is less than a hundred songs per year.

3. The years chosen at random were 1932 (28), 1946 (41), 1951 (34), 1961 (263), 1974 (160), 1985 (172), and 1997 (78).

4. Stolorow and Atwood (1992) give exact parity to self and relationship, and Gergen and MacNamee (1999) come close to doing so. These two books look toward a relational psychology, and therefore to integration between psychology and the social sciences.

5. Two supplementary studies of charted romance lyrics in less modernized societies suggest that they have more and stronger exceptions currently than the U.S. Erika Moreno (2000) found 7 exception Spanish language lyrics in the charts of Spain and Costa Rica in 1999 alone. One of these was strongly exceptional, involving four concrete characteristics of the beloved. Frank Ha (2000) has found that charted Korean heartbreak lyrics tend to emphasize the beloved's pain more than the lover's, suggesting alienation in the engulfed mode, rather than the isolation of Western romance lyrics. Both of these findings provide preliminary support for the theory of social integration proposed here.

CHAPTER 5

NOBODY KNOWS
BUT ME

Curtailment of Feeling

This chapter concerns changes in attitudes toward emotions in the lyrics of Top 40 popular songs ushered in by the '60s. The number of emotion words decreased, and lyrics that directly described or displayed curtailment of feeling increased. Although there were a few of these types of songs before 1958, the rapidity and intensity of the changes presents something of a puzzle. This chapter will describe a new breed of songs, and discuss possible causes for the change.

Chapter 4 proposed that there was an increase in alienation in Top 40 lyrics beginning in the sixties. This change was part of a gradual increase that began in the '30s and continued through the 70 years of lyrics in the study reported in the last chapter. Even if we compare individualism in lyrics in the '30s and the '90s, the amount of difference, gradually increasing in the intervening years, is still not great. Compared with the massive changes that took place in the lyrics and music of the Top 40 in the '60s, the changes in the degree of individualism over the entire 70 years are all but overshadowed. However, the abruptness of the appearance of lyrics of direct curtailment is commensurate with the dramatic changes of musical forms in the '60s.

The historians of the '60s refer to the change as a "cultural revolution" in Western countries, one that was brought about by young people. In a detailed account of changes in youth culture in France, Italy, Germany, and the United States, Marwick (1998) shows that the changes in the period that we refer to as "the sixties" actually began in 1958 in these four countries.

The first of the romance songs describing blatant curtailment of emotion occurs in the Top 40 of 1958:

> And when I smile, it's just a pose
> My heart is breaking but no one knows
> ("No One Knows")

A similar description of curtailment in a song with a similar title ("Nobody Knows" 1996).

> I pretended I'm glad you went away
> … I'm dying inside and nobody knows it but me

As indicated below, there have been many such lyrics in the Top 40 since 1958.

Also absent from the earlier period are lyrics that renounce all feeling, like those in "What's Love Got to Do with It?" ("Who needs a heart when a heart can be broken?" 1984) and "I Am a Rock" (Simon and Garfunkel 1965):

> I have no need of friendship; friendship causes pain.
> It's laughter and it's loving I disdain.

Curtailment

Theorists have argued that modern civilization curtails the expression of emotion. For Freud (1930) civilization was tantamount to repression of feeling and desire. In this vein, Freud had many followers, such as Reich, Marcuse, and others. Elias (2000) was spectacularly more specific, showing that modernization curtailed expression of anger and therefore aggression, at least in face-to-face encounters.

At the very core of his thesis, Elias also proposed that although shame and embarrassment were increasingly used as methods of social control their outward expression was being flagrantly curtailed.

Another widely held thesis asserts a historical shift from shame to guilt (Benedict 1934). It is not clear in this view whether shame is repressed in favor of guilt, or guilt merely replaces shame.

Finally, it has been proposed that curtailment of the expression of shame leads to either withdrawal and depression or angry violence and other pathologies (Gaylin 1984; Scheff 1994; Elias 1996; Gilligan 1996). This idea suggests an inverse correlation between changes in the rates of violent crime and the expression of shame. The curtailment hypothesis is a very general statement about social process in modern civilizations.

Most of these ideas have been stated only in broad terms, and with only illustrative evidence. The most systematic documentation was by Elias (2000), because he analyzed "minute particulars," excerpts from advice manuals in five European languages over a span of seven centuries.

The hypothesis that *modern civilization curtails the expression of emotion*, if true, could be important in many areas, such as child-rearing, psychotherapy, education, crime control, and conflict resolution. Psychotherapy, for example, is divided between schools of thought that emphasize emotion (e.g., psychoanalysis, catharsis, Gestalt) and those that do not (e.g., behaviorist, cognitive, and narrative therapies). Findings supporting the curtailment hypothesis might imply support for the emotion-oriented therapies, as well as changes in other areas.

Another example: managing intense emotions is a key concern in resolving protracted conflict. Yet most current training and literature on mediation and conflict resolution gives very little attention to emotions, perhaps making mediation less effective than it could be (Retzinger and Scheff 2000).

Besides Elias, I have found only one study that seriously attempts to document the curtailment thesis, a historical study of attitudes toward anger in the United States over the last two centuries (Stearns and Stearns 1986). They examined a very large number of texts, including advice manuals, diaries, and secondary studies. Their findings support the hypothesis with regard to anger. They report that early in the nineteenth century, only excessive anger was condemned. Righteous anger was not only not condemned, but even encouraged. Toward the middle of the nineteenth century, however, they suggest that intolerance of any kind of anger began to arise, and continues, increasingly, into the twentieth century.

The Stearnses admit that their study had many shortcomings. For example, they mention "inability to establish the representativeness of any given source" and lack of explicit coding procedures ("Often the researcher is forced to reason from brief comments on subtopics (e.g. temper tantrums), circumlocutions, ... and from the outright absence of comment where it should be logically expected" [1986, p. 249]). The names of most of the many documents they examined are not stated or even enumerated, and the method of coding anger not made explicit. For these and other reasons, the reliability of their findings cannot be assessed. Another limitation of the Stearns's study is that it concerns only anger, leaving out other emotions. Unlike Elias, for whom the rising threshold against the expression of shame was a key feature of the civilizing process, the Stearnses have little to say about shame, its siblings and cousins like embarrassment, humiliation, guilt, envy, etc., or, for that matter, independent emotions like grief, fear, pride, and love. Expert opinion now holds that the various emotions interact, particularly anger with the shame family, contempt and disgust. If we are to study changes in emotional expression, it would be advantageous to include several emotions, not just one. Determining simultaneous historical changes in several emotions could discriminate between various theses. For example, has there been a shift from shame to guilt, or decreasing expression of all the emotions?

As indicated in Chapter 3, it appears that lyrics for the period 1930–1958 were much more likely to mention emotion and feeling names than later lyrics (e.g., "With each word your tenderness grows, tearing my fear apart ... " "The Way You Look Tonight" 1936). The present study addresses another aspect of the repression thesis, increases in direct curtailment of emotions.

Types of Curtailment Lyrics

Lyrics which involved direct references to curtailment of feeling were rare in the Top 40 before 1958, but plentiful since then. There were only a few such songs before 1958.

> I'm laughing on the outside, crying on the inside
> Cause I'm still in love with you.
> ("Laughing on the Outside" 1946)

Another example is "Pretend" (1953):

> Pretend you're happy when you're blue
> It isn't very hard to do

And a similar lyric from 1956, "The Great Pretender":

> My need is such I pretend too much
> I'm lonely but no one can tell

However, in the '30s, there were also indirect and abstract expressions of curtailment. Many of these songs proposed that one deals with painful emotions (being "blue") by hiding them.

> Keep your sunny side up, up!
> Hide the side that gets blue.
> ("Sunny Side Up" 1930)

The following lyric make a similar suggestion. It also suggests that the appearance of such lyrics at this time may be related to the Great Depression, which began in 1929.

> Leave your worries on the doorstep
> Life can be so sweet on the sunny side of the street
> ("On the Sunny Side of the Street" 1934)

Another famous lyric may have addressed war and its aftermath rather than the Depression:

> You've got to accentuate the positive
> Eliminate the negative
> ("Ac-cent-tchu-ate the Positive" 1945)

Another example:

> Things never are as bad as they seem
> So dream, dream, dream.
> ("Dream When You're Feeling Blue" 1945)

These four lyrics, and others like them, expressed the curtailment of painful feelings as a goal, but in a very general way. These lyrics are indirect, because no particularly painful emotions are mentioned and no suffering is described. They advise the curtailment of feeling, but in a way that is itself curtailed.

Direct descriptions of curtailment of feeling began to be frequent in 1958. They come in two types. The first involves open descriptions of curtailment, often by the singer. Some of these lyrics have already been mentioned in earlier chapters:

> Everywhere people stare
> Each and every day
> ("You've Got to Hide Your Love Away" 1965)

The same idea is expressed in many subsequent lyrics, like "The Tracks of My Tears" (1967):

> My smile is my makeup
> I wear since my breakup with you

This passage suggests curtailment in a way that is subtle, at least for popular lyrics: a close look will show that the smile that the singer is wearing is not genuine, but false.

Heartbreak in these types of songs is about two different kinds of suffering: the pain of loss, and the pain of hiding the pain of loss, as in the Beatles song.

Several songs express curtailment, but only with respect to one person, the beloved:

> He's got me smiling when I should be ashamed.
> Got me laughing when my heart is in pain.
> ("A Fool in Love" 1960)

The second type of curtailment song that appeared in the sixties doesn't *tell* about curtailment, but *shows* it in the lyrics themselves. An example is provided by one of Bob Dylan's most popular songs ("Don't Think Twice, It's All Right" [1967]):

> I ain't sayin' you treated me unkind,
> you could have done better but I don't mind
> You just kinda wasted my precious time,
> but don't think twice, it's all right

This song veils anger and hostility in irony and sarcasm. The vast gap between the expression of good will and anger is especially flagrant.

A slightly different kind of curtailment, of positive emotions in order to avoid negative emotions, is implied in another of the biggest of the '60s hits, "I Am a Rock":

> I am a rock, I am an island
> And a rock feels no pain, and an island never cries.

An entirely different kind of song can also be found before the sixties, but is absent afterwards: a lyric that advises against curtailment:

If your sweetheart sends a letter of goodbye
It's no secret you'll feel better if you cry
("Cry" 1952)

This type of lyric is all but unknown after 1958, when curtailment, rather than expression of emotions, becomes the norm.

Conclusion

In Top 40 lyrics there seems to have been a dramatic change in attitudes toward the expression of emotions in 1958. Before that year, there were a few lyrics that described the curtailment of emotional expression directly, and a few more that counseled it abstractly and indirectly. But beginning in 1958, there followed a large number of lyrics that described or displayed curtailment directly and in detail. This change might be taken to reflect a trend toward greater repression in modern societies. If that is the case, then the cultural revolution of the '60s was in part a move toward liberalizing politics, but was at the same time moving in a conservative direction in terms of emotions.

CHAPTER 6

GENUINE LOVE AND CONNECTEDNESS

Everyone already knows that romantic love requires sexual attraction; that's a given. The second component is almost as well known. It's called attachment, and it's part of the show in both romantic and all other kinds of love, including love within families. Attachment is found in other mammals besides us humans: our cats Mischa and Wolfie have become attached to me and my wife, Suzanne Retzinger, and we are attached to them.

Attachment gives a physical sense of a connection to the beloved. The most obvious cues to attachment are missing the beloved when she or he is away, and contentment when she or he returns. Loss of that person invokes deep sadness and grief. Another less reliable cue is the sense of having always known a person whom we have just met. This feeling can be intense when it occurs, but it also may be completely absent.

Attachment accounts for an otherwise puzzling aspect of "love": one can "love" someone that one doesn't even like. A popular

song from the '40s, "I Don't Know Why (I Just Do)," evokes this
kind of "love":

You never seem to want my romancing.
The only time you hold me is when we're dancing.

These lyrics from 1962 have the same idea: "I don't like you but I
love you. / Seems that I'm always thinking of you" ("You've Really
Got a Hold on Me"). One is attached, despite oneself, and regardless
of the other's behavior, no matter how rejecting. Attachment, like
hunger, thirst, and sexual desire, is at root a physical reaction.
Attachment gives the lover a sense of urgency, even desperation. Furthermore, attachment is like imprinting in non-human
creatures; in its pristine form, it occurs very early in infancy,
and may last a lifetime. It is attachment that makes loss of a
loved one profoundly painful. After such a loss, one may grieve
for many months or years. Grief is the price that we pay for lost
attachment.

Finally, there is a third component that is much more complex
and subtle than attraction or attachment. It has to do with the lover
sharing the thoughts and feelings of the beloved. The lover identifies with the loved person at times, to the point of actually sharing
thoughts and feelings. He or she feels the beloved's pain at these times,
or joy, or any other feeling, as if it were his or her own. Two people can
be attuned, at least at times, to each other's thoughts and feelings.

It is important to note, however, that to qualify as genuine
love, the sharing needs to be balanced between self and other. One
shares the other's thoughts and feelings as much as one's own, no
more and no less.

The sharing of consciousness with the lover, unlike attachment, varies from moment to moment. Closeness and distance
alternate, reaffirming not only the union, but also the individual

autonomy of each member of the pair. The idea of the love bond as involving continuous attachment, on the one hand, but also varying amounts of closeness and separation, solves a critical problem in the meaning of love. The bestseller *Women Who Love Too Much* (1985) describes continuing relationships with husbands who are abusive of wife or children, or both.

The women profess that they can't leave these men because they love them too much. Since the word *love* is used so broadly in English, this usage is perfectly proper. Yet these kinds of relationships fail the test in terms of the way love is being defined here, because they lack balance between self and other. The wife identifies with the husband much, much more than he identifies with her. The wives are *engulfed* with their husbands. In these cases, the word *love* serves as denial of pathological dependency and/or passivity.

In terms of the idea presented here, these wives are at least attached to their husbands, and may also be sexually attracted to them. But it is clear that the third component, identification, is not balanced in the sense of equally representing self and husband in their thinking and feeling. The husband counts too much, the wife too little. What the wife feels is not genuine romantic love, because it lacks equality of mutual identification.

Lust, infatuation, and dependency represent orientations that are often confused with love. This confusion may help to hide the separation and isolation that is characteristic of our society. Our society focuses on, and rewards, self-reliant, separate individuals to the point that all social bonds, not just love, are at risk.

Applications

The definition of romantic love proposed here involves three components, *the three A's*: Attraction, Attachment, and Attunement.

To the extent that this concept is an advance over other definitions, what practical application might it have? One implication concerns the possibility of change in each of the three underlying dimensions. The first two, attachment and attraction, are largely involuntary and constant. They are more or less given and fixed. But the third parameter, degree of shared identity and awareness, may be open to change through communication.

Communication creates a bridge between persons. In a love relationship it can increase shared awareness and balance shared identity so that it is roughly equal on both sides, over the long run. That is, although one partner might be valuing the other's experience more (or less) than her own in a particular situation, momentary isolation or engulfment could be managed over the long term so that the experience of each partner, on the average, is equally valued in the relationships. This issue comes up continually, especially in marriage: the dialectic between being two independent persons, on the one hand, and being a we, on the other: "I-ness" and "We-ness."

Partners seldom complain about too much "We-ness," although it is just as much of a problem as too little. It is customary to interpret engulfment with another person as closeness, or with a group as loyalty or patriotism. An eminent person I met at a party told me "I am a patriot; I do whatever my country tells me." But engulfment leads to problems down the road. Unless both parties can contribute their own unique point of view, a kind of blindness ensues that inhibits cooperation and effectiveness, and in the long run, morality.

On the other hand, too little "We-ness" is usually seen as a problem. A now divorced friend told me that the last straw was when her husband forgot he was supposed to meet her when her ocean liner docked. She said, "I was never in his head." Isolation between partners is highly visible, at least to the one whose point of view is not being valued.

A second issue that is dependent on effective communication is shared awareness. Skillful communication and observation can lead to revealing the self to the other, and understanding the other. This issue is particularly crucial in the area of needs, desires, and emotions. By the time we are adults, most of us have learned to hide our needs, desires, and feelings from others, and to some extent, perhaps, even from ourselves. We develop automatic routines that obscure who we are. Long-term love relationships require that these practices be unlearned, so that we become *transparent* to our partner and to ourselves. Unlike attachment and attraction, frequent and skillful communication can improve the balance in shared identity, and increase shared and individual awareness.

Especially in arguments and quarrels, it is crucial to use "I" messages, revealing one's own motives, thoughts, and feelings, rather than attributing them to the other person. This practice usually helps find resolution of conflict. On the other hand, the opposite practice, attributing negative motives, thoughts, and feelings to the other, shame and blame, usually increases it. You did this and you did that, you, you, you ... is a path toward alienation.

The practice of "leveling," being *direct* but *respectful* (Satir 1972), is a step toward effective communication. It is easy enough to be respectful without being direct, or direct without being respectful. But respectful assertiveness is a stretch for most of us. By using these and other communication practices, love, which is usually thought of as given, may be increased.

One final issue, the degree of attunement, needs further discussion. The definition of love offered to this point hasn't specified one issue that might be important for practical reasons. How near to exact equality must the empathy and identification of each partner with the other be to qualify as love? All that has been said so far is that the amount should average out, over the long term, to near equality. But how near?

Exact equality of empathy between partners might exist in a few moments, but even there it would be rare. Usually one partner is more empathic and values the other's point of view more than the partner does in reverse. In terms of my definition, does this mean that the more empathic partner loves more? Not necessarily; it may only mean that the more empathic person is engulfed with the other.

Even if the relationship is unbalanced, compensatory actions are possible. One such move could involve what might be called secondary attunement. If the less empathic partner becomes aware that he is understood better by his partner than he understands her, and that he identifies less with her than she does with him, he can compensate in other ways. For example, by listening longer to her than she does to him. Direct attunement is important in a relationship, but it is by no means the whole story, just as attachment and attraction are not the whole story either. Adult relationships are so complex that the three A's provide only a preliminary and tentative definition of love, to stimulate discussion.

Six Kinds of "Love"

Table 6.1 is a graphic representation to help visualize the kinds of non-erotic "love" not included in the new definition. It helps clarify two of the three basic dimensions and how they give rise to a definition of LOVE and its look-alikes.

Of the kinds of non-erotic "love" represented in this table, only one represents LOVE as it is defined here: #2. The other

Table 6.1 LOVE and Its Look-Alikes

Non-erotic "Love"

Attunement (shared identity and awareness)

	Self-Focus	Balance	Other-Focus
Attach.	1. Isolated obsession	2. LOVE	3. Obsess. Idealization.
Not att.	4. Isolated interest	5. Affection	6. Idealization

five cells represent affects that are often confused with love. This confusion, as already mentioned, may help to hide the painful separation that is characteristic of our society. Discussion of the five types of pseudo-love can help to flesh out the idea embedded in the proposed definition.

Parental feeling toward an infant usually involves non-erotic, one-way LOVE (cell 2). The parents will be strongly attached to the infant at the moment of birth, or even beforehand, and the infant to the parents and other caretakers, but LOVE means not only attachment, but also attunement. Very early in the infant's life, however, the caretaker can learn to understand aspects of the infant's experience by accurately interpreting body language and cries (Stern 1977). Perhaps during the first week, the caretaker is able to experience one-way non-erotic love toward the infant.

Granting that strong attachment between infant and parent begins at birth, the infant cannot return the LOVE of the parent because it is unable to become cognitively and emotionally attuned to the parent. The parent and other caretakers must teach the infant how.

Some of this process has been described by Bruner (1983). The mother holds the doll in front of the baby's face, saying, "See the pretty dolly." Her intention is only to teach the name of the object. But inadvertently, she is also teaching the child joint attention (attunement). After many repetitions, since the child sees that the mom is looking at the dolly and referring to it, the child senses that the doll is not only in its own mind, it's also in the mom's mind. Completing this process takes many years. Children vary considerably, but at some point between the fifth and eighth year, the child becomes able to take the role of the parent to the point that it becomes interdependent, rather than dependent.

However, the beginnings of mutual attunement seem to occur long before the development of language. Tronic et al (1982) have documented the exchange of smiles between infant and caretaker after only several months. Quite properly, according to the definition of love offered here, they refer to this process as "falling in love." From the moment of birth, the infant and the mother are intensely attached. Exchanging of mutual glances and smiles begins the other component of non-erotic mutual love, attunement. The infant and caretaker must learn to look, then look away, rather than stare. When both learn to smile in response to the look, they are taking the first step toward LOVE, because each senses the feeling of the other.

The cells in Table 6.1 can also represent romantic love if the component of sexual attraction is added. With this change, then cell #2 would represent one-way romantic LOVE. Perhaps the emotion of the Helen Hunt character toward the Nicholson character in *As Good as It Gets* is of this type. She is evidently attracted and attached to him, and is able to share his point of view. But since he is unable to share hers, her LOVE for him is not returned. The affect he holds for her might be represented by #1. With sexual desire added, this cell could be named isolated desire or infatuation. He is apparently attached and attracted to her, but is trapped within himself, to the point that he is not sufficiently aware of her thoughts and feelings.

Another variation on this kind of relationship is represented in *Remains of the Day.* The butler (played by Anthony Hopkins) is very competent in his job, but his emotions are completely suppressed. He is attracted to the house manager (played by Emma Thompson), and she to him. But they cannot connect because his emotional blankness rules out attunement. She cannot understand his feelings, because he hides them.

Non-erotic affection (#2) is characteristic of most stages of effective psychotherapy. In the film *Good Will Hunting,* Will, the patient, doesn't understand or identify with Sean, the therapist (played by Robin Williams), until a session near the end of their meetings.

But Sean rapidly learns to understand Will. He shows his understanding in the crucial session. Sean knows from Will's dossier, and from his disclosures, that Will suffered brutal physical abuse as a child. Sean tells Will, "It's not your fault." This phrase, when repeated many times, breaks down Will's resistance to experiencing his emotions. Will has said nothing about feeling that the abuse was his own fault. Because of his experience as a therapist, Sean is able to "read Will's mind." That is, to be attuned with Will in the sense of identifying with him and understanding even those feelings which are hidden.

In most successful therapies, the patient becomes highly attached to the therapist, but without understanding the therapist (#4, isolated interest, or #6, idealization, depending on the patient's style of relating).

An instance of #5, non-erotic affection, but toward a group of persons, is represented in climactic scene of the extraordinary French/Danish film *Babette's Feast.* The film takes place in 1869, after a wave of repression in France. Babette, a world-class French chef, is in political exile. Her husband and children have been killed, and she herself is in danger. A mutual friend has arranged for her to be taken in as a cook by two elderly sisters in a small village in Denmark. Her thoughts and feelings are completely unknown to the sisters and the villagers. Ordinarily, she prepares the simple food for the sisters that is customary in their village. But when she wins a lottery, she uses all of the money to prepare a feast, a last chance to be an artist, to bring to the village the wonder of art.

The villagers hugely enjoy the feast, but except for one out-sider, they have no idea what they are being exposed to, nor, for that matter, who Babette is and the great art she represents. Babette's understanding of the villagers, and their lack of awareness and un-derstanding of her, gives the episode of the feast a poignancy that is both humorous and tragic.

It has been claimed (Goddard 1951; Evans 1960; Scheff 1979) that shared awareness (and its absence) among the characters within the play, and between audience and the characters, is the key feature of all drama: it is what provides drama in the theatre. Evans (1960) calls misunderstandings "discrepant awareness." I (1979) have proposed that discrepant and shared awareness are the fundamental components of "distance" in drama: aesthetic distance, like the attunement in genuine love, involves a balance in the audience's perspective, being equally involved in and detached from the drama.

Cell 1 characterizes most cases of intense jealousy, a pseudo-love. Jealousy, like infatuation (to be discussed below), often is mostly fantasy. In Shakespeare's play *The Winter's Tale*, King Le-ontes needed no Iago to spur his jealousy, or even any indication that his queen (Hermione) desired another. It was entirely a fantasy. The king was not attuned with Hermione, although she was with him, a failure of mutual attunement.

The core emotions in jealousy derive from the response to real or imagined rejection (shame) by the loved one, and anger toward the rival. If there is attachment (in cell 1), jealous desire is obsessive. If there is little attachment (#1 or 3), there is still sexual desire but little or no obsession. The key to overcoming jealousy may lie in the way the shame component is managed. If it is acknowledged freely, both shame and anger will be diminished. But if the shame is not acknowledged, as is especially the case with most jealous men, the shame and anger may spiral out of control, as represented by Leontes in *The Winter's Tale* and in "crimes of passion."

One-way desire without attachment or attunement is represented in #4 and 6. A man who desires a particular prostitute, but is not attached or attuned, would be an example. If she were not available, he might desire another equally. #1 and 3 represent the situation in which he becomes attached to her, adding obsession to his desire for her. In the film *Pretty Woman*, as in many others, at first the character played by Richard Gere is only attracted to the prostitute played by Julia Roberts, as in #4. As he gets to know her, he also realizes that he misses her when they are apart, as in #1. Finally he marries her, although the degree of his attunement with her is not clear. As in most commercial films and novels, little evidence is offered about the degree of attunement.

Infatuation

Most laypeople and many scholars think of infatuation as a rehearsal for love, or at least marriage, as suggested in most romantic films. However, as already indicated in Chapter 5, there are other possibilities. It may be more likely that an infatuation will continue at that level, with the same or different persons. Infatuation, with or without attachment, seems to be much more common than genuine love.

Obsessive non-erotic idealization is represented in #3 and 1. In families, a child may idealize one or both parents or a sibling, and be so attached that this person or persons occupies their attention. Idealization of kin is only part of an important pattern in many families. The other half is vilification. Often there is a triangle in which two persons idealize or vilify another family member. A common pattern is a coalition between the child and one parent against the other. Both vilification and idealization can create havoc in the family.

This pattern is represented in Shakespeare's *King Lear*, but it takes the form that the king mistakenly idealizes his two older daughters but vilifies his youngest. Since the two older daughters flatter him for their own ends, and the youngest refuses to because she is direct and honest, the play shows how he is made to suffer because of his obliviousness.

#3 represents non-attached idealization. In a group of friends, one may idealize one or more of the friends. With sexual attraction #3 represents light infatuation. Mutual infatuation seems to occur often among high school and college students, judging by their comments. Since both parties anticipate rejection, it may not lead to an actual contact.

It is important to emphasize the difference between romantic infatuation and LOVE, since the two are often confused, even by scholars of romance. Woody Allen's film *The Purple Rose of Cairo* has a scene that is emblematic of this kind of desire. The heroine, played by Mia Farrow, is a constant filmgoer. To escape from her husband's brutality, she has been spending her spare time in the movie house, viewing a single long-playing romantic film over and over. She "falls in love" with one of the characters, played by Jeff

Daniels. She is only mildly surprised when he jumps out of the screen to talk to her. She is telling the friend how wonderful he is: kind, gentle, attentive, etc. The friend says, "But Mary, he isn't real." The Mia Farrow character answers, "You can't have everything."

Infatuation can involve both attachment and attraction, but there is insufficient attunement. As in the case with Mia Farrow's character, the desire is less for a real person than for an imagined one. Attunement requires contact with the real person, so that one can understand her thoughts and feelings. Infatuation requires very little contact, or even none. Indeed, contact with the real person may reveal that she or he has thoughts and feelings that are unwelcome, and bring an abrupt end to desire.

#1 can represent mutual obsession where there is attachment. This arrangement usually leads to conflict if the two parties frequently interact and/or depend on each other. To the extent that each focuses on self rather than other, little learning takes place in the relationship; they bounce off each other like billiard balls. #4 represents a similar situation, but without obsessive attachment, the conflict may be at a lower level of frequency and intensity. How these relations are played out depends to a large extent on the style of response by the other party.

#5 represents a relationship that might be unusual: non-erotic mutual attunement without attachment. Perhaps there are friendships like this. One is fond of another whom one also understands, but without urgency. Perhaps there are marriages or affairs in which the two parties understand and are attracted to each other, but with little attachment, as in #5. Again, how this relationship proceeds will be dependent on the response style of the other party.

#3 comes closest to representing the relationship between Cathy and Heathcliff in *Wuthering Heights*. Judging from the portrayal of them in the novel, they are obsessively and erotically engulfed with each other. This idea of requited "love" can also be found in many other novels and in the lyrics of popular songs. Similarly, one-way obsessive, erotic infatuation is often called love in novels and popular songs. Another similar combination is unrequited romantic love. Perhaps the love of the Helen Hunt character toward the Nicholson character in *As Good as It Gets*, already mentioned above, is of this type. She is evidently attracted and attached to him, and is able to share his point of view. But since he is unable to do the latter, her love for him is not returned. Like an infant, he cannot partake of and value her point of view as much as his own. The affect he holds for her might be called obsessive desire. He is apparently attached and attracted to her, but tends toward self-focus, rather than balance between self and other. This cell also characterizes most cases of intense jealousy, which is also a pseudo-love.

The Effect of Hidden Emotions on Relationships

Most of the affects referred to as pseudo-love may be generated by the denial of specific emotions, such as grief, anger, and especially shame. Chapter 2, on concepts of emotion, provided an explanation of why a certain kind of shame is an especially crucial impediment to genuine love.

What I call the pride/shame conjecture has three parts: 1. All interaction with others, even imagined interaction, requires us to see ourselves from the point of view of the other. 2. Yet seeing ourselves from the point of view of the other generates either pride or shame/ embarrassment. 3. For that reason, the issue of managing these emotions is present in most human contact. Even without contact, this dynamic may be played out over and over with imagined others.

If emotions are managed by shunting them aside, as they usually are in Western societies, they disrupt the experience of other emotions. *Unacknowledged shame/embarrassment often leads to either hostility or withdrawal* (Lewis 1971; Scheff 1990, 1994, 1997; Retzinger 1991; Tangney and Dearing 2002), which in turn impedes or deflects the experience of love.

A scene in the film *Big* provides a humorous example of the way shame/embarrassment may be masked with hostility. In the film Tom Hanks plays the part of a 10-year-old boy who is magically living in the body of a grown man. In one scene, a grown woman is coming on to the man, but initially Hanks's character doesn't understand. When it finally dawns on him that it means that she likes him, Hanks gives the woman a playground shove.

The way that young boys are socialized to hide their embarrassment or shame behind hostility and aggression is captured in this harmless moment. It is less funny in the actions of street gangs and leaders of nations. In modern societies, both men and women tend to routinely lose track of their emotions, creating a crisis of alienation.

Any kind of relationship that involves attachment, attunement, or attraction to any degree, no matter how much hostility or withdrawal are involved, is seen in an alienated society as preferable to no relationship at all. This tendency obfuscates and confuses. As one step toward decreasing our confusion, a narrow definition of love like the 3 A's offered here may help.

Summary

To the extent that the definition of love proposed here proves useful, what practical application might it have? One implication concerns the possibility of change in each of the three underlying dimensions. The first two dimensions, attachment and attraction, are largely physical and constant. It is not clear how these two dimensions might be intentionally changed. The third parameter, however, degree of shared identity and awareness, is open to change through skillful communication practices.

One goal of communication between persons in a love relationship would be to balance the level of shared identity so that it is roughly equal on both sides, over the long run. That is, although one partner might be valuing the other's experience more than her own in a particular situation, momentary isolation or engulfment could be managed over the long term so that the experience of each partner, on the average, is equally valued in the relationships. This issue comes up continually, especially in marriage: the dialectic between being two independent persons and being a we, "I-ness" and "We-ness."

This poem by Marge Piercy seems to be grappling with the problem of a balanced relationship:

> To Have Without Holding
> Learning to love differently is hard,
> It hurts to thwart the reflexes
> of grab, of clutch; to love and let
> go again and again as we make and unmake in passionate
> diastole and systole the rhythm
> of our unbound bonding, to have
> and not to hold, to love
> with minimized malice, hunger
> and anger moment by moment balanced.

A second issue that is dependent on effective communication is shared awareness. Frequent and effective communication can lead to revealing the self to the other, and understanding the other. This issue is particularly crucial in the area of needs, desires, and emotions. By the time we are adults, most of us have learned to hide our needs, desires, and feelings from others, and to a large extent, even from ourselves. Long-term love relationships seem to require that these practices be unlearned, so that we become *transparent* to our partner and to ourselves. Unlike the extent of attachment and attraction, effective and frequent communication can improve the balance in shared identity, and increase shared awareness.

Can the three dimensions of love be observed, so as to be identified in discourse? The two physical variables, attachment and attraction, would not pose a problem. But identifying the degree of shared awareness and identity would. There is a large literature on what is called Interpersonal Perception that might be one place to start. The difficulty with these studies is that they are mostly static and cannot be used to give dynamic assessments of the state of the bond. There are also by now some studies of "I-ness and We-ness"[1] in relationships that might be more immediately helpful, especially those based on recorded dialogue.

Conclusion

This chapter has suggested that the mindlessly broad definition of love in modern societies is a defense against feeling the painful emotions that are generated in the social-emotional world. The notion that love is sacred and/or indescribable can also function to defend ourselves against the pain of loss, separation, or alienation.

The explicit definition of genuine love proposed here might help discover the emotions disguised by vernacular usage, and the kinds of dysfunctional relationships that are hidden under the many meanings of love. The next chapter takes up an issue that turns out to be parallel to the problem of defining genuine love: What is the meaning of the word *shame* and its cognates and near kin in current usage, and what should it be?

Note

1. Carrere, S., Buehlman, K. T., Coan, J. A. Gottman, J. M., Coan, J. A., Ruckstuhl, L. (January 2000) Predicting Marital Stability and Divorce in Newlywed Couples, *Journal of Family Psychology*, 14, No. l, pgs. 1–17; Fergus, K. D., & Reid, D. W. (2001) The couple's mutual identity. *Journal of Psychotherapy Integration* 11(3), 385–410. The former article offers an empirical approach to mutual identity, the latter article a theoretical approach.

CHAPTER 7

WHAT EMOTION IS THE SHADOW OF LOVE?

The title of this chapter was inspired by a song (2004) by the English punk-rock singer P. J. Harvey: "Shame Is the Shadow of Love"

> Tried to go forward with my life
> I just feel shame, shame, shame ...

Although shrewd and attractive, this song has never made it to the Top 40, even in England, and probably never will, for reasons to be discussed below.

The language of emotion in the most popular love song lyrics is vastly misleading. The images of love, on the one hand, and shame, on the other, seem particularly distorted. As already discussed in Chapters 2 and 3, the meaning of love is so broad that it refers to many kinds of relationships, including dysfunctional or imaginary ones. This chapter will describe another important confusion, how shame is implied frequently in romance lyrics, but so indirectly as to be virtually invisible. The lyrics of popular songs often hint at shame, but its presence is almost never acknowledged. In recent years experts on emotions have begun to note that shame is usually hidden in modern societies. The psychologist Gershen Kaufman proposed that it is taboo to mention this emotion, just as direct reference to sex was forbidden in the nineteenth century: "American society is a shame-based culture, but ... shame remains hidden. Since there is shame about shame, it remains under taboo." (Kaufman 1989)

Another psychologist, Helen Lewis (1971), had earlier found supporting evidence in her study of emotions in hundreds of psychotherapy sessions. Using a systematic coding system for emotion words and phrases, she found that shame or embarrassment were by far the most frequent emotions, occurring in most sessions, and repeatedly in some. Nevertheless their presence was hardly ever mentioned by either the patient or the therapist. As indicated by Kaufman's comment about our society, there seemed to have been "shame about shame" not only in the patient, but surprisingly also in the therapist. In these sessions, shame was "the elephant in the room."

As already indicated in the earlier chapters, shame is not the only elephant, but perhaps the most hidden one. The next section will suggest why it is important that emotions be brought out into the light of day.

Why Are Emotions So Important, Even in Popular Love Songs?

Experts agree that emotion and feeling are important for many reasons. However, there may be a reason so far little mentioned that is concerned with their relationship to thought: emotions serve to distinguish what is important to the individual from myriads of cognitions that are not.

This idea was illustrated in Chapter 1 by my own experience with visitors to an Iraq War Memorial installed every Sunday by the Veterans for Peace. Emotions and feelings, even weak ones, serve as indicators of what is significant. The visitors to the war memorial already knew that a large number of U.S. soldiers had died in Iraq, but until they *felt* its meaning, it was just one of many meaningless numbers.

Unlike the intergalactic universe of cognitions, the domain of emotion and feeling is quite small. There may be only a dozen or so true emotions, culturally universal, genetically determined states of bodily arousal (such as those mentioned in Chapter 2, love, fear, grief, anger, and shame). There are more affects, emotion and cognition combinations, with the emotion part strong (jealousy, vengefulness, etc.), say fifty. Finally there is a still larger domain of feelings, also a cognition/ emotion combination, but with the emotion component weak, often a mere tinge (e.g., nostalgia). Perhaps there are hundreds of these.

Hospice workers report that most family networks quickly become intolerant of normal grieving, and that mourners may be given psychiatric drugs to stop their crying. In medical research, emotions are usually portrayed as the enemy. Not just anger, but also grief, fear, and shame.

In the fast pace of hypercognized societies, one learns that there is "No Time to Cry" (Iris Dement 1993).

My father died a year ago today,
The rooster started crowing when they carried Dad away
...
I've got no time to see
the pieces of my heart that have been ripped away from me.

The intolerance of authentic emotions and mass hypercognition together may be the main reason that the need for meaning can be exploited. Mass entertainment, popular music, and commercial films usually follow mechanical formulas that arouse emotions. Most popular songs attract attention not because of their art, but because they target feelings of love and loss. Horror films, similarly, arouse fear. Action films both arouse and justify the affect of vengeance. Mass entertainment seems to be popular to the extent that it arouses emotions, even mechanically.

Political exploitation of the need for meaning through emotion may be a similar device. The fraudulent marketing of the Iraq war was probably successful because it played on and amplified the fear and vengefulness in the public that resulted from 9/11. Perhaps manipulation of the public will continue as long as authentic emotions are lost in a sea of cognition.

Shame, the Missing Emotion

Top 40 songs illustrate the idea of a taboo on shame, as well as a vast overuse of the word *love*, as indicated earlier. This chapter will propose that heartbreak songs, particularly, represent emotions in this way. On the one hand, heartbreak and infatuation are taken to indicate love. As indicated in earlier chapters, infatuation is mostly a fantasy; there is usually little or no relationship, only projection onto another person not actually known. Similarly, lyrics about heartbreak represent it as showing intense love. Yet there are often suggestions that what is being represented is not so much love but obsession, unresolved grief, or pathological dependency:

> And I can't keep picturing you with him,
> And it hurts so bad, yeah

...

I can't take it yeah, I can't shake it ("Over and Over" 2004)

Taking this kind of preoccupation as evidence of love casts it in a favorable light. A less favorable interpretation would be to see it as a product of the inability to mourn. The last line, particularly, portrays an insoluble dilemma: continuing pain that might be experienced as unbearable. What are the emotions that could cause such agony?

Grief and/or anger are clearly implied in most heartbreak lyrics. These emotions seem to be less taboo both in lyrics and in the larger society. On the other hand, references to embarrassment, shame, and humiliation, although frequent, are usually hidden or indirect, as seems to be the custom in our society. It is possible that these latter emotions, when not acknowledged, can lead a shadow life, underlying and amplifying emotions to the point that one's feelings are experienced as unbearable. The idea of amplification of feeling will be further discussed below.

A great majority of Top 40 songs concern love and romance, more than three quarters, year after year. Chapter 2 described the three largest categories in the U.S. Top 40: heartbreak, infatuation, and requited love. In the order mentioned, these patterns were stable over the 70 years from 1930 to 2000. Other kinds of love songs also occur, but much less frequently, such as those about sexual attraction or, very rarely, a loss with little pain or acrimony.

The Language of Heartbreak

As indicated in earlier chapters, the single largest category of love songs is the heartbreak of loss, about 25 percent of all Top 40 songs, year after year. They all involve an extreme situation, loss of the loved one, usually because of rejection. Less extreme situations, such as those that don't involve complete loss and/or rejection, are seldom considered. Emotional pain within requited love, for example, is seldom considered. Many heartbreak songs are straightforwardly about the kind of complete and dramatic loss that gives rise to intense grief.

Yet, as indicated earlier, there are still other kinds of emotion implied in addition to grief and anger. Although the word *shame* is not mentioned, these lyrics transparently convey the public shame, embarrassment, and humiliation of being rejected.

> Feeling two foot small, everywhere people stare
> I can see them laugh at me
> ("You've Got to Hide Your Love Away" 1968)

Many heartbreak songs imply shame but still less obviously.

> I thought that bein' strong meant never losin' your self-control
> But I'm just drunk enough to let go of my pain,
> To hell with my pride, let it fall like rain
> ("Tonight I Wanna Cry" 2004)

The phrase about pride is a common way of implying shame indirectly. It refers to the embarrassment most men experience if they cry or even feel like crying. Men are trained to believe that crying is unmanly.

In this lyric, shame is implied more strongly:

> I pretended I'm glad you went away,
> These four walls closin' more every day
> And I'm dying inside, and nobody knows it but me
> ("Nobody Knows" 1996)

The only direct indication of emotion is to grief ("crying inside"). It is used, however, to imply not only grief but also shame: the pain of rejection is so shameful that it must be hidden from others. The last three lyrics are strongly indicative of the curtailment of emotions, which was the topic of an earlier chapter.

Since the word *shame* sometimes occurs in Top 40 lyrics, even in titles, one might think the emotion of shame is being represented. However, "Ain't it a shame" and similar phrases do not actually refer to emotion. A similar phrase, "What a shame!" occurs in everyday conversation, but it is without emotional content, since the same meaning can be conveyed by "What a pity!" In modern societies, direct references to the emotional meaning of shame are infrequent.

The song "Shame" mentioned above is a rare exception. It is not widely known, at least in the United States, but it seems to imply that feelings of shame inevitably accompany genuine love. This song names the emotion that so many songs hide, and hints at its close association with love.

This lyric refers to heartbreak, the pain of being left by one's lover. But unlike other heartbreak lyrics, this one does not suggest grief or anger. Rather it openly names shame as the emotion that is causing suffering. Cleverly, in lines not shown here, the song also uses the word *shame* in a vernacular way, "It's a shame."

The main emotional risk of loving may be not only the desperate grief of dramatic loss. The song by Harvey recognizes shame, as well as grief, as the master emotions in romantic relationships. Shame is the shadow of love. This observation may point to the answer to a difficult question concerning emotional pain. How can it be experienced as unbearable?

The quotation by Kaufman that is mentioned earlier in this chapter may provide a hint. "Since there is shame about shame, it remains under taboo" (1989). Although Kaufman didn't expand on the idea of "shame about shame," it might imply an explanation of unbearable emotional pain. The idea that one can be ashamed of being ashamed suggests that shame, particularly, can loop back on itself, amplifying the original feeling without limit.

The predicament of persons who blush easily from embarrassment provides an illustration. Students who blush easily when they are embarrassed have told me that whatever the source of the original feeling, their blush further embarrasses them; they become acutely self-conscious. Although the reaction may stop after only one loop, some of them have experienced lengthy cycles of continuing self-amplification. Indeed, one of my informants, a professional actor, recounted an incident which got out of hand. During a rehearsal, he began blushing because of mistakes he was making in his lines. The more self-conscious he became, the more he blushed, ending in paralysis to the point he had to be carried off stage.

On the other hand, it was also clear from some of the informants' stories that acknowledging their embarrassment, especially when it led to laughter, quickly brought an end to the vicious circle. It would appear that pain that seems continuous and/or unbearable is caused by denial. The more the person denies, the more the emotion can interfere with self-control. Shame is inevitably the shadow of love. Yet it causes serious consequences only when it is continuously and routinely denied.

The hiding of shame in song lyrics provides a language for the listeners that can help them deny their own shame and that of others in real life. This practice seems to both reflect and reinforce the denial of emotion in the larger society.

To sum up: emphasis on extreme situations and disguising shame ignores the many subtle emotional risks that accompany even requited love. For example, whether the relationship is short or long, loving someone more, even slightly more, than they love you can give rise to shame. Another possibility is that in loving another person, one becomes more susceptible to their disdain.

Jealousy is one obvious example of the risks involved in loving. The slightest hints of detachment can trigger it. For example, you and your lover are talking to your friend at a party about a film all three of you have seen. For a few seconds, you notice that your lover and your friend are making eye contact with each other as they excitedly talk about the film, but not with you. You feel excluded, if only briefly, but enough to trigger your jealousy. For that brief period, you feel intense pains of betrayal by your lover, and anger, even hatred, toward the friend.

In the same situation, if you are very secure in your relationship, you probably wouldn't feel jealousy. However, it might still be painful. Being excluded from eye contact can evoke momentary shame, no matter how secure the relationship.

Close relationships can be much more comforting, but also much more upsetting than other relationships. Most Top 40 popular songs provide an idealized and therefore unrealistic picture of love. It is portrayed as a safe haven from all pain, which it is not. It both protects from and generates emotional pain.

The last chapter of this book will consider some possible responses to emotions in songs and in life other than complete denial. As already indicated above, acknowledgment seems to be a much more helpful reaction than denial. The next chapter describes and summarizes the implications of this study for understanding both popular songs and real life.

CHAPTER 8

THE BEAT
GOES ON

Alienation and Curtailment of Emotions

What have we learned about popular song lyrics in this book? The first part of this chapter will summarize the patterns of love lyrics that have persisted over the last eighty years, and how each pattern represents and evokes the social-emotional world. The second part discusses implications of these findings, particularly the dysfunctional role these songs might play in the lives of listeners. Finally, ways that the songs might be changed are proposed, and the possibility that these changes might help to change our society.

Heartbreak, Infatuation, and Requited Love

Over the years, the most common Top 40 love song has always been heartbreak, loss of the beloved. The next most common is a miscellany of romance songs, some of which might be seen as stories or comedy or at least unusual. Increasingly, some of the lyrics in this category are about sex, often quite explicitly. The next most common is infatuation, being "in love" with a person who is hardly known, if at all. Finally, the least common lyric concerns requited love, having a beloved who returns one's love.

In the typical heartbreak lyric, the loss of the beloved causes intense pain, sometimes to the point that it is portrayed as unbearable. Being unable to go on without the lost lover is another way of putting it, or that one's life is ruined or made worthless by the breakup. Angrily blaming the lost one for the split-up is common, either alone or in conjunction with the lover's suffering.

Many lyrics that are not taken up completely with pain and suffering and are optimistic about the future can't resist a few resentful comments about the ex-beloved. The expression of anger may be somewhat muted, but nevertheless obvious, as in these lines excerpted from "Better in Time" (Leona Lewis 2007):

> If you didn't notice, boy, you mean everything to me ...
> Was it all that easy, to just put aside your feelings? ...

This lyric is unusual in its insistence on working out the breakup and being optimistic about the future, yet three lines imply resentment against the lost one: the two lines above and the phrase *hurt my feelings* (which implies a complaint: YOU hurt my feelings). In this instance, the resentment, however muted, raises doubts about the working through. Instead the lover seems to be reassuring herself, perhaps to hide her underlying emotions.

There is also a clear contradiction between the words and the music that raises doubts. The main text is almost a ballad, but the rhythm is too fast for this form. The beat of the chorus is still faster and more emphatic. The overall effect mixes calm words and agitating music. This song is not an ideal model for surviving heartbreak through effective mourning.

Infatuation lyrics report love at a distance from its object. Often, the love object has only been seen, not actually met. Even if talk has occurred, it doesn't convey the real feelings of the lover. The classic "I've Told Every Little Star" (1932) portrays the situation:

> I've told every little star
> Just how sweet I think you are, why haven't I told you?

The kind of love that is usually portrayed as infatuation might just as readily be termed obsession. In many of the lyrics, it is portrayed as exhilarating. But others describe dysfunction, instead of, or in addition to, obsession: "Crazy About Her" (1989) involves a litany of suffering:

> Can't get a good night's sleep, ain't been to work in weeks ...
> Can't get her off my mind, I'm drinking too much wine,
> I'm burning up inside ...

The least frequent category of Top 40 love lyrics is requited love. "No One" (2007) by Alicia Keys is an example.

> No one ... Can get in the way of what I feel for you
> I know people will try to divide something so real ...

This lyric has most of the characteristics of the typical requited love song, such as being focused entirely in an abstract, unclear way on the lover's thoughts and feeling, with nothing about the beloved's, nor any realistic image of the beloved. Even though seemingly about requited love, the content suggests that the lover is somewhat isolated from the beloved. It also has another theme, the lovers against all others, us against them. That is, even if the lovers as a pair are connected, they are alienated from everyone else.

The most obvious emotion represented in heartbreak lyrics is grief, although this term is never used. However, a closely related word, *sad* or *sadness*, is sometimes mentioned. Heartbreak lyrics frequently refer to tears and crying, usually an indicator of grief and mourning. Mostly, however, these lyrics spell out the unrelieved pain and suffering of unresolved grief. In real life, tears and crying, and indeed the whole process of mourning, need not be extremely or at least constantly painful. At optimal distance, going rapidly back and forth toward the earlier grief and the present safety, crying can be pleasant, "a good cry" (distancing of emotions was discussed in Chapter 3).

The same process of distancing works as well for shame, fear, and even anger as it does for grief. It can be done alone, but is much facilitated by having a good listener, someone who will provide a patient and non-judgmental ear for whatever time it takes. Successful mourning often requires not only grief work but also shame, anger, and/or fear work as well.

Anger is obviously represented in many heartbreak songs, indirectly or directly. In some of these lyrics, anger takes over entirely, with little or no indication of grief. Most often, however, as in real life, the indications of anger are muted, as was the case with "Better in Time," discussed above.

Finally, many heartbreak lyrics represent a third emotion, but quite indirectly. The shadowy presence of this emotion, shame, was discussed in Chapter 6. Shame can be the dominant emotion in a lyric, yet its presence is only implied. An example quoted in an earlier chapter is "Nobody Knows" (1996), in which the shame references are more muted than in the Beatles lyric "You've Got to Hide Your Love Away" that was discussed in Chapter 7.

The pain is real even if nobody knows,
Now I'm dyin' inside
And nobody knows it but me.

There is a reference to grief ("crying inside") but the main emotion seems to be shame ("dying inside," [as in mortified, a surrogate for shame] "like a clown," and "pain"). There is also an implication of social isolation ("four walls closing"), a relational reference, that will be discussed below.

In modern societies, shame mostly goes hidden or at least unacknowledged, and not just in love lyrics. The expression of all emotions is curtailed in modern societies, as discussed in Chapter 5, as well as shame. Anger might at first seem an exception, since it is often acted out with great intensity. Yet, as is the case with other emotions, most anger is probably curtailed in order to keep the peace, and for many other reasons as well.

The Relational World

If, as suggested in Chapter 6, being connected with the thoughts and feelings of the beloved is a key component of genuine love, then very few Top 40 love lyrics are about love. The failure of connection is most obvious with infatuation lyrics, since the lover usually has barely met the beloved, if even that. Lacking a real connection, the lover fantasizes hopes about how the beloved might be, but is lost in his or her own head.

Most heartbreak songs also show a lack of connection with the beloved. Like infatuation lyrics, they tend to be almost entirely about the lover, his or her suffering, desperation, and in many cases, anger and/or shame. The beloved's thoughts and feelings are seldom mentioned.

Furthermore, the image of the beloved is usually a tissue of abstractions, with very few particulars that would suggest a real person. Even at the height of positive feelings, the beloved is portrayed only abstractly, as beautiful, gorgeous, without compare, and so on, suggesting that the lover might be self-absorbed, rather than aware of the beloved as a person. Surprisingly, this pattern is found not only in heartbreak and infatuation lyrics, but even in most songs about requited love.

Here are two exceptions from the usual pattern, in which at least one particular about the person or the moment is described:

> I love how your eyes close whenever you kiss me
> ("I Love How You Love Me" 1961)

This is not just one moment, but it does portray a concrete particular about the beloved, that she closes her eyes when she kisses her lover.

These lines from "The Lady in Red" (1986) describe both a moment and an image that are highly particularized:

> I've never seen you shine so bright, …
> I have never seen that dress you're wearing
> *Or the highlights in your hair that catch your eyes …*

As already indicated, however, most of the love lyrics in this study do not particularize the beloved. Instead, the picture is a composite of abstract virtues, in the case of infatuation and requited love, or, in some of the heartbreak lyrics, abstract vices. The poet-artist William Blake wrote: "Art and science cannot exist but in minutely organized particulars" (c.1803–1820, Ch. 3, plate 55, line 60). If he was right, then the typical popular love lyric is neither art nor science.

Another relational problem with the typical love lyric is that it tends to focus narrowly and obsessively on the loved one only, excluding any connection with a larger group or community. This pattern was referred to earlier as being like Bonnie and Clyde (you and me against the whole world).

To find love lyrics that expand, rather than constrict, the lover's connections, one has to reach back some fifty years to a lyric already mentioned in Chapter 4, "Til There Was You" (1957):

> There were bells on the hills but I never heard them ringing
> I never heard them at all til there was you.

"Everybody Loves a Lover" (1958) expresses this idea perfectly:

> And I love everybody ...
> Since I fell in love with you

These lyrics are in direct contrast to the typical love lyric, since they describe connecting with a larger whole, as well as loving a single person. They particularly contrast with the lyrics of the type that emphasize the pair of lovers against the whole world (to be further discussed below).

Models of Genuine Love

Are there any Top 40 lyrics that come close to modeling genuine love? The requirements discussed above insure that there will be none, since they are so numerous and demanding. However, there is one classic lyric that contains many desirable features, and another that comes even closer, showing all the features except one. Both lyrics were mentioned in Chapter 4, but the treatment of them here will be somewhat different. Both are from virtually the same year in the '30s.

"These Foolish Things" (1936) contains some of the features of a model experience of loss and mourning.

The ties that bound us are still around us
There's no escape that I can see
And still those little things remain
That bring me happiness or pain ...
A cigarette that bears a lipstick's traces
An airline ticket to romantic places
And still my heart has wings
These foolish things remind me of you
A tinkling piano in the next apartment
Those stumbling words that told you what my heart meant
A fairground's painted swings
These foolish things remind me of you ...
How strange, how sweet, to find you still
These things are dear to me
They seem to bring you near to me
The winds of March that make my heart a dancer
A telephone that rings but who's to answer
Oh, how the ghost of you clings
These foolish things remind me of you.

This lyric is clearly awash with particulars, like "A cigarette that bears a lipstick's traces." There is no hint of anger or resentment. The words are mostly about pleasure, rather than pain, such as "How strange, how sweet, to find you still. / These things are dear to me. / They seem to bring you near to me."

On the other hand, there are some elements that don't fit. On the emotion side, there is the line "And still those little things remain, that bring me happiness or *pain*." And in this connection, there is one of the particular moments that might bring back a painful memory: "A telephone that rings but who's to answer?" which suggests a connection missed.

There are many particulars in the lyrics, but they are all about moments and objects, not about the lost beloved. There is no image of the lost one at all. All of the particulars are indirect, in that they evoke memories of the beloved, but none of them help provide an image of her.

The next example, "They Can't Take That Away from Me" (1937) comes very close to meeting all the requirements.

> ... They may take you from me, I'll miss your fond caress.
> But though they take you from me, I'll still possess:
> The way **you wear your hat**
> The way **you sip your tea**
> The memory of all that
> No, no, they can't take that away from me
> The way **your smile just beams**
> The way **you sing off key**
> The way you haunt my dreams
> No, no, they can't take that away from me
> ... I'll always, always keep the memory of:
> The way **you hold your knife**
> The way **we danced till three** ...

It is an art song, like the last example, in that it has many particulars, but in this case, they are all about the beloved. There is even a negative particular, singing off key, that helps bring the loved one to life as an actual person, not an idealized image. There is only one particular that is not about the beloved, but it is a particular moment ("The way we danced til three").

Both the lyrics and the music suggest pleasure rather than pain. Even though the relationship no longer exists, the lover is grateful for it, the memories are still a source of pleasure. The major thing that is missing to make this lyric a model of completed mourning is the expansion of the lover's vision; like most love lyrics, the focus is entirely on the beloved.

In fact, one of the sub-themes, "they can't take that away from me," is just a whisper of what has become a roar today, us against the whole world, the focus on the beloved to the exclusion of everyone else. This was the theme of "Bleeding Love" (2008), the biggest hit of the year.

> But I don't care what they say
> I'm in love with you

The theme of *us against them*, only one of several themes in "They Can't Take That Away from Me" (1937) and "No One" (2007, discussed above), has become dominant in "Bleeding Love" and other recent hits.

These lyrics, like virtually all Top 40 love songs, are focused narrowly on the loved one, excluding any larger community. This kind of relationship was discussed in Chapter 1 under the heading of the engulfed form of alienation (too close). It is found in almost all Top 40 love lyrics.

The lyrics under discussion above also involve the opposite type of alienation, isolation (too far), since they flagrantly oppose the outside world. The lovers, as a group, are portrayed as isolated from all other groups. The combination of engulfment within a group and isolation from outside groups can be called bimodal alienation: engulfment within, isolation without (Scheff 1994). It involves one of the most complete alienations from self and others that can be imagined.

Alternatives to Infatuation

The classic lyric "They Can't Take That Away from Me" comes close to modeling an ideal heartbreak lyric. Except for enlarging the lover's reach to include a larger world, it contains all of the other desirable characteristics. What about a model of the ideal infatuation lyric? Does one exist?

I searched titles for a desirable model. As a starter, I searched the line: "I want to get to know you better ... ," hoping to find follow-up lines in a form similar to this:

> (Hypothetical lyric): I am very attracted to you, but I want us to move slowly enough so that we get to know each other. I have done the instant head-over-heels before, many, many times, and it hasn't worked for me. If we get close enough to understand each other's thoughts and feelings, maybe our relationship would have a chance.

Alas, no such luck. There were five current lyrics that start with the line "I want to get to know you better," but none of them comes remotely near the hypothetical. Indeed, the first lyric I found followed up "I want to get to know you better" with an obscenity: "So I can fuck you."

For comic relief, here is an example of a pattern in a film as an alternative to infatuated behavior. In *P.S. I Love You*, the character played by Lisa Kudrow apparently had been the victim of many earlier infatuations. So when she saw a man that seemed cute to her, she was ready to test his likely compatibility with a series of test questions, if necessary. The first was: "Are you married?" In the first instance shown, when he said yes, she turned away.

At the next party, she questioned another cute man: "Are you married?" He said no. She then asked: "Are you gay?" When he said yes, she turned away. At still another party, with yet another cute man, she got negatives to both questions. She kissed him on the mouth, then turned away.

Finally, at another gathering with another man, she got negatives to both questions, and didn't turn away after kissing him. In fact, in the film she went on to marry him. In this instance, at least, she would not be a victim of pure infatuation. But in popular love lyrics I could find nothing remotely like a test of infatuation.

Almost all of the requited love lyrics lack desirable characteristics. Even those that have one or more still lack others. "Lady in Red" (1986) mentioned above particularizes the beloved and also portrays particular moments, and can again be used as an example. Like most love lyrics, it focuses entirely on the couple relationship, isolated from the larger world. The setting is a dance with many others dancing around them:

> I've never seen so many people want to be there by your side
> And when you turned to me and smiled
> It took my breath away

Yet the lover rejects them:

> There's nobody here ...
> It's just you and me.

Even the best of the Top 40 could use some improvements.

Steps Toward More Helpful Lyrics

The following list of basic areas of change summarizes the suggestions of earlier chapters under two headings: emotions and relationships.

Emotional Issues

Acknowledging rather than curtailing emotions. The lyrics could invoke grief, joy, pride, shame, anger, and other emotions directly, rather than indirectly through euphemisms, or omitting all or most of the emotions that should accompany close relationships.

1. Using the word LOVE more carefully, excluding infatuation, lust, and many other attitudes with which it is often confused.
2. Heartbreak: working through grief instead of basking in it. Example, having "a good cry" instead of an unbearably painful one (see earlier chapters on optimal distance). The lyric "They Can't Take That Away from Me," discussed above, offers a model of resolved grief.
3. Anger: finding and verbalizing the underlying feelings rather than acting them out. Referring directly to anger rather than using sarcasm and other hiding devices. A model beginning for acknowledging anger in the real world would start with "I am angry at you because.... "
4. Acknowledging rather than hiding shame, embarrassment, and humiliation as the "shadow of love." Using shame terms

directly rather than euphemisms (Chapter 7). The model lyric in this case is "Shame Is the Shadow of Love."

Relational Issues

The new lyrics should try to show a realistic picture of desirable relationships between lovers, rather than only implying it or omitting it entirely.

1. Particularizing the beloved with at least one detailed image and/or particular moment, rather than resorting to only abstractions (beautiful, desirable, beyond compare, etc). Once again, "They Can't Take That Away from Me" provides details that evoke an image of the loved one as an actual person.

2. Infatuation: questioning its authenticity, rather than getting lost in it. Testing the reality of one's infatuations, as the Lisa Kudrow character did in *P.S. I Love You*.

3. Sexuality: relating to romance and the emotion of love rather than just sex, and gender equality rather than sexism.

4. At least some indication of connectedness, in the sense of deep knowledge of the loved one by the lover, and of the lover by the loved one. Here is an example from an art song: "In the slow world of dreams, we breath in unison. The outside dies within, and she knows all I am" (the poem "Memory," by Theodore Roethke was put to music by Ned Rorem. Suggested to me by Charles Bazerman).

5. Showing how love can expand one's views and attachments, rather than narrowing them down to only the beloved.

The idea in this poem that the loved one knows ALL he is, a strong allusion to the unity of lovers. Example: "Everybody Loves a Lover" (1958).

Nine improvable areas give the lyric writer considerable scope for creating new kinds of love songs. Is it possible that young people, with a little help from social science, could create love songs that are art rather than kitsch, or at least functional rather than dysfunctional? The Afterword speaks to this issue.

Love does not have to be merely a secondhand emotion ("What's Love Got to Do with It?").

If understood properly, love can have everything to do with it.

AFTERWORD

Two Projects for Better Lyrics

It would be extremely difficult to change the pattern of alienation that dominates popular love songs, since it both reflects and generates the social-emotional status quo in the larger society. What follows will be for the purpose of encouraging discussion: two tentative suggestions that might be steps in the right direction. The first would be establishing **classes on popular songs in high schools and colleges;** the second, closely related, would be **contests for writing better lyrics.** The classes would in effect be like training for the contests.

Classes: Popular Songs and Life

A class about popular songs might work best with high school seniors and college freshmen. My experience with college freshmen clearly showed that most were deeply interested in popular songs. Their interest came very close to being a religion with many of them, since popular songs have intense personal meanings; they are, so to speak, sacred. The purpose of the class would be to help the students compare the songs they love with real life, and in doing so, learn a little about social science and about real life emotions/ relationships. Even students who are not particularly interested in popular songs might be attracted to the course as a vacation from the usual required classes.

Ideally, the class would have a *discussion* format, with no lectures. The main class activity would be an open discussion of the lyrics of selected popular songs, using *role-playing* based on the lyrics, as discussed below. The students could email the teacher one of their favorite romance lyrics before each class meeting. The teacher could choose the lyrics that are most popular and/or would be the most useful for comparing songs with their own lives. It would be important that the name of the student who contributed the lyric be strictly anonymous. Because of the searching nature of the class discussions, if students' choices were identified, they might become anxious about contributing lyrics that they actually liked.

For the first assignment, the students would be asked to choose a favorite song that is a duet between the lover and the loved one. This duet would be the basis for a series of role-plays, with students volunteering to play the roles. In the first few role-plays, the students would stick to the script in the lyric. After warming up in this way, they would be encouraged to invent different kinds of responses to each of the roles in the lyric. These invented lyrics give rise to laughter and intense interest. For that reason, the role-playing becomes fun, as well as educational.

In subsequent assignments, students are encouraged to choose their favorite lyrics, but invent a voice for the beloved, responding to the role of the singer of the lyric. This step allows the class to take on a creative quality that the students might find enjoyable and useful.

The teacher would help the students to bring out the implications of the lyrics, especially the way emotions and relationships are represented, and how the situations described might be changed in real life. In the lively discussion that ensues, the students might get ideas about the realities of love and romance. The teacher would also comment on the relationship of the lyrics, both real and invented, to major concepts in the social and behavioral sciences—for example, the way in which a heartbreak lyric implies alienation. Students comment that the concrete examples of dialogue seem to bring sociology or psychology to life.

This book could serve as a manual for the teachers, but a much shorter and simplified book would be available as a textbook for the students. It would briefly outline the basic lyric patterns on the Top 40 and the representations and distortions of emotions and relationships in most lyrics. In this way, some popular songs could become art songs, as well as being popular. Over the years, the students in the many classes I taught on Communicating, which were also a way of teaching about emotions and relationships, were surprised and grateful about what they learned about real life. A constant refrain in their course evaluations was that the class was unlike anything they had ever learned at home or in a school, since it had immediate value for them in their own lives. A popular song class could fill a similar function, but for a much wider audience.

Lyrics Writing Contest

The courses described above could lay the groundwork for a yearly contest for new song lyrics. It would begin by being only local, but to the extent that it is successful, might expand to state and national levels. It might even become a reality show on TV. Cash awards would be made, of course, for the most creative and attractive lyrics.

Guaranteed airtime would also be part of the prizes. The winning lyrics would need to be creative and attractive. Yet they would also point toward unalienated love and acknowledged emotions, in a way that the overwhelming majority of past lyrics have not.

REFERENCES

Ainsworth, Mary, M. Blehar, E. Waters, and S. Wall. 1978. *Patterns of Attachment*. Hillsdale, NJ: Lawrence Erlbaum Associates.

American Heritage Dictionary of the English Language, Third Edition. 1992. Boston: Houghton Mifflin.

Anderson, Benedict. 1991. *Imagined Communities: Reflections on the Origin and Spread of Nationalism*. New York: Verson.

Andreas Capellanas. 1969. *The Art of Courtly Love*. New York: Norton.

Baumeister, R. F., and M. R. Leary. 1995. "The Need to Belong: Desire for Interpersonal Attachments as a Fundamental Human Motivation." *Psychological Bulletin* 117: 497–529.

Benedict, Ruth. 1934. *Patterns of Culture*. New York: Houghton Mifflin.

Blake, William. 1964 [c.1803–1820]. *Jerusalem*. Barnes and Noble.

Bloom, Harold. 1998. *Shakespeare: The Invention of the Human*. New York: Riverhead Books.

Bowlby, John. 1969. *Attachment and Loss*. V. 1. New York: Basic Books.

Bruner, Jerome. 1983. *Child's Talk*. New York: Norton.

Buss, David. 1994. *The Evolution of Desire*. New York: Basic Books.

Christenson, Peter, and Donald Roberts. 1998. *Its Not Only Rock and Roll: Popular Music in the Lives of Adolescents*. Cresskill, NJ: Hampton Press.

Colin, Virginia. 1996. *Human Attachment*. Philadelphia: Temple University Press.

Cooley, Charles H. 1922. *Human Nature and the Social Order*. New York: Scribner's.

Dewey, John. 1925. *Experience and Nature*. New York: Dover (1958).

Edwards, Emily. 1994. "Does Love Really Stink?: The Mean World of Love and Sex in Popular Music of the 1980s" in Jonathan Epstein (Editor), *Adolescents and Their Music*. New York: Garland Publishing.

Elias, Norbert. 1987. *The Society of Individuals*. Oxford: Blackwell.

————. *The Germans: Power Struggles in the Nineteenth and Twentieth Centuries*. New York: Columbia University Press.

————. 1998. *On Civilization, Knowledge, and Power: Selected Writings*. Chicago: University of Chicago Press.

————. 2000. *The Civilizing Process*. Revised ed. Oxford: Blackwell.

————. 1972. *What is Sociology?* London: Hutcheson.

Evans, Bertrand. 1960. *Shakespeare's Comedies*. London: Oxford University Press.

Fisher, Helen E. 1992. *Anatomy of Love: The Natural History of Monogamy, Adultery, and Divorce*. New York: Norton.

Freud, Sigmund. 1915. "Observations on Transference-Love." *Standard Edition*. 12.

————. 1930. *Civilization and Its Discontents*. London: Hogarth Press.

Frith, Simon. 1996. *Performing Rites*. Cambridge, MA: Harvard.

————. 2007. *Taking Popular Music Seriously*. Burlington, VT: Ashgate.

Gaylin, Willard. 1984. *The Rage Within: Anger in Modern Life*. New York: Simon and Schuster.

Gergen, Kenneth, and Sheila MacNamee. 1999. *Relational Responsibility*. Thousand Oaks, CA: Sage.

Gilligan, James. 1996. *Violence: Reflections on a National Epidemic*. New York: Vintage.

Goddard, Harold. 1951. *The Meaning of Shakespeare*. Chicago: University of Chicago Press.

Goffman, Erving. 1959. *Presentation of Self in Everyday Life*. New York: Anchor.

Ha, Frank. 2000. Personal correspondence.

Hatfield, Elaine, and R. L. Rapson. 1993. *Love, Sex, and Intimacy*. New York: HarperCollins.

Horton, Donald. 1957. "The Dialogue of Courtship in Popular Songs." *American Journal of Sociology* 62: 569–578.

Izard, Carroll. 1977. *Human Emotions*. New York: Plenum.

Johnson, Rolf. 2001. *Three Faces of Love*. De Kalb, IL: Northern Illinois University Press.

Kaufman, Gershen. 1989. *The Psychology of Shame*. New York: Springer.

Kemper, Theodore. 1978. *A Social-Interactional Theory of Emotions*. New York: Wiley.

Kemper, Theodore, and Muriel Reid. 1997. "Love and Liking in the Attraction and Maintenance Phases of Long-term Relationships." *Social Perpectives on Emotions*. 4: 37–69.

Krystal, H. 1988. *Integration and Self-Healing: Affect, Trauma, Alexithymia*. Hillsdale, NJ: Analytic Press.

Levine, Peter A. 1997. *Waking the Tiger: Healing Trauma*. Berkeley, Calif.: North Atlantic Books.

Lewis, Helen B. 1971. *Shame and Guilt in Neurosis*. New York: International Universities Press.

Lewis, Thomas, Fari Amini, and Richard Lannon. 2000. *A General Theory of Love*. New York: Random House.

Lyrics World. 2000. http://www.summer.com.br/percent7Epfilho/html/top40/index.html.

Marwick, Arthur. 1998. *The Sixties: Cultural Revolution in Britain, France, Italy and the United States, 1958–1974*. Oxford: Oxford University Press.

Metge, Joan. 1986. *In and Out of Touch*. Wellington, NZ: Victoria University Press.

Miller, William. 1993. *Humiliation*. Ithaca: Cornell U. Press.

Moreno, Erica. 2000. "A comparison of Top 40 Spanish and English Language Romance Lyrics in 1999," unpublished paper.

Nagel, Thomas. 1979. "Sexual Perversion." Chapter 4 in his *Mortal Questions*. Cambridge: Cambridge University Press.

Nussbaum, Martha. 2001. *Upheavals of Thought: The Intelligence of Emotions*. Cambridge: Cambridge University Press.

Ortega y Gasset, José. 1957. *On Love*. New York: Meridian.

Ortony, Andrew, Gerald Clore, and Allan Collins. 1988. *The Cognitive Structure of Emotions*. New York: Cambridge University Press.

Persons, Ethel. 1988. *Dreams of Love and Fateful Encounters*. New York: Penguin.

Plutchik, Robert. 2003. *Emotions and Life*. Washington, D.C.: American Psychological Association.

Puente, Sylvia, and Dov Cohen. 2003. "Jealousy and the Meaning of Love." *Personality and Social Psychology Bulletin* 29: 449–460.

Retzinger, Suzanne. 1991. *Violent Emotions: Shame and Rage in Marital Quarrels.* Newbury Park: Sage.

———. 1995. "Identifying Shame and Anger in Discourse." *American Behavioral Scientist* 38: 541–559.

Retzinger, S., and T. Scheff. 2000. "Emotion, alienation, and narratives: resolving intractable conflict." *Mediation Quarterly* 7: 3–19.

Rosenberg, Marshall B. 1999. *Nonviolent Communication.* Del Mar, CA: PuddleDancer Press.

Rougemont, Denis de. 1940. *Love in the Western World.* New York: Harcourt Brace.

Satir, Virginia. 1972. *Peoplemaking.* Palo Alto: Science and Behavior Books.

Scheff, Thomas. 1979. *Catharsis in Healing, Ritual, and, Drama.* Berkeley: University of California Press.

———. 1990. *Microsociology: Discourse, Emotion, and Social Structure.* Chicago: University of Chicago Press.

———. 1994. *Bloody Revenge: Emotions, Nationalism, and War.* Boulder, CO: Westview.

———. 1997. *Emotions, the Social Bond, and Human Reality.* Cambridge: Cambridge University Press.

———. 2001. "Words of Love and Isolation in Pop Songs." *Soundscapes: Online Journal of Media Culture.* 4 (Oct.).1–17.

———. 2007. "Hidden Emotions: Responses to a War Memorial." *Peace and Conflict: Journal of Peace Psychology.* 13 (2) 1–9.

Seeman, Melvin. 1975. "Alienation Studies." *Annual Review of Sociology* 1: 91–124.

Shackelford, Todd K. 1998. "Divorce as a consequence of spousal infidelity." In Victor de Munck (Editor), *Romantic Love and Sexual Behavior.* Westport, Conn.: Praeger.

Shaver, Philip, and C. Clark. 1994. "The psychodynamics of adult romantic attachment." In J. Masling and R. Bornstein (Editors), *Empirical Perspectives on Object Relations Theory.* Washington, DC: American Psychological Association.

Shaver, Philip, S. Wu, and J. C. Schwartz. 1992. "Cross-cultural similarities and differences in emotion and its representation: A prototype approach." In M. S. Clark (Editors), *Emotion* (pp. 175–212). Newbury Park: Sage.

Soble, Alan. 1990. *The Structure of Love.* New Haven: Yale University Press.

Solomon, Robert. 1976. *The Passions*. New York: Doubleday.
———. 1981. *Love: emotion, myth, and metaphor*. Garden City, NY: Anchor Press/Doubleday.
———. 1992. *About Love: Re-inventing Romance for Our Times*. Lanham, Md.: Littlefield Adams.
Stearns, Peter, and Carol Stearns. 1986. *Anger: The Struggle for Emotional Control in America's History*. Chicago: Chicago University Press.
Stendhal, 1975. *Love*. London: Penguin.
Stern, Daniel. 1977. *The First Relationship*. Cambridge: Harvard University Press.
Sternberg, Robert. 1988. "Triangulating Love." In Sternberg, R. and M. L. Barnes (Editors), *The Psychology of Love*. New Haven, Conn.: Yale University Press.
Stolorow, Robert, and George Atwood. 1992. *Contexts of Being: The Intersubjective Foundations of Psychological Life*. Hillsdale, NJ: Analytic Press.
Sullivan, Harry S. 1945. *Conceptions of Modern Psychiatry*. Washington, DC: W. A. White Foundation.
Tangney, June, and Rhona Dearing. 2002 *Shame and Guilt*. New York: Guildford Press.
Tennov, Dorothy. 1979. *Love and Limerance*. Chelsea, MI: Scarborough House.
Tomkins, Silvan S. 1963. *Affect, Imagery, Consciousness*. Vol. l. New York: Springer.
Tronick, E., M. Ricks, and J. Cohen. 1982. "Maternal and Infant Affect Exchange." In T. Field and A. Fogel (eds.), *Emotion and Early Interaction*. Hillsdale, NJ: Lawrence Erlbaum.
Volkan, V. D. 1988. *The Need to Have Enemies and Allies: From Clinical Practice to International Relationships*. Northvale, NJ: J. Aronson, Inc.
———. 1997. *Bloodlines: From Ethnic Pride to Ethnic Terrorism*. New York: Farrar, Straus and Giroux.
———. 2004. *Blind Trust: Large Groups and Their Leaders in Times of Crisis and Terror*. Charlottesville, VA: Pitchstone Publishing.

INDEX

"Ac-cent-tchu-ate the Positive," 98
"Addicted to Love," 68–69
adulation, 24
aesthetic distance, 112
Affect/Imagery/Consciousness
   (Tomkins), 51
affection, non-erotic, 111
aggravation, 53
alienation: bimodal, 141;
   connectedness and, 81–82;
   defined, 14; forms of, 82;
   heartbreak and, 131–135;
   increase in, 93; infatuation
   and, 131–135; isolation as,
   14, 82; requited love and,
   131–135; in romance lyrics, 75;
   social integration and, 82–90;
   solidarity and, 35–41, 84, 87–88
Allen, Woody, 114
"Almost Like Being in Love," 75
amplification of feelings, 125
"Angel Baby," 72
anger: attitudes toward, 96;
   emotion language of, 49; in
   heartbreak lyrics, 7–8, 125, 132,
   134; helpful lyrics about, 143;
   righteous, 96; signs, 55t

angerworld, 28
anxiety, 47–48, 54
apologies, 55
arguments, 107
As Good as It Gets, 33–34, 110,
   116
assertiveness, 107
attachment: infatuation and, 115;
   romantic love and, 103; sadness
   and, 39–40; theory, 26–27; to
   therapist, 111
attraction. *See* sexual attraction
attunement: connectedness and,
   31–32, 37–38; defined, 25;
   degree of, 107–108; direct, 108;
   importance of, 37–38; between
   infants and caretakers, 81;
   infatuation and, 115; mutual,
   110–112; non-erotic love
   and, 109t; parental, 109–110;
   romantic love and, 104–105;
   secondary, 108
audience, 57, 112
autonomy, connectedness *v.*, 30

Babette's Feast, 111–112
ballads, 84–85

basic emotions, 45
The Beatles, 63–64, 79, 99, 134
beliefs, emotions and, 10–13
beloved, image of, 79–80, 136, 144
"The Best Things in Life Are
    Free," 80
"Better in Time" (Lewis, Leona),
    87, 132, 134
Big, 117
bimodal alienation, 141
Blake, William, 136
"Bleeding Love," 140
Bloom, Harold, 19
blushing, 128
"Bobby's Girl," 69
bodily resonance, 26

"Can't Let Go," 77
"Can't Take My Eyes Off You," 72
Capellanas, Andreas, 22
capitalism, 83
"Cherie Amour," 64
classes, on popular songs, 147–149
closeness, 14
close relationships, 129
cognitions, emotions *v.*, 11–12
commercial films, emotions
    aroused by, 12
commitment, 38
communication: goals of, 118;
    limbic, 26, 46; shared awareness
    dependent on, 107, 118–119;
    shared identity changed by, 106
compulsion, 67, 76–77
conflict resolution, 96
connectedness: alienation and,
    81–82; attunement and,
    31–32, 37–38; autonomy *v.*,
    30; empathetic, 37–38; failure

of, 135; genuine love and,
    103–120; heartbreak lyrics and,
    135–136; in helpful lyrics, 144;
    importance of, 13–14, 37–38
consciousness, intersubjective,
    31–32, 81–82, 104
constricted view, 74–76, 137
Cooley, C. H., 31, 58
"Crazy," 66
"Crazy About Her," 66, 70, 133
crimes of passion, 113
"Cry," 7, 101
crying, 126, 134
cultural revolution, 94
curtailment of feeling: abrupt
    appearance of, 94; in heartbreak
    lyrics, 7–8, 78; lyric types,
    97–101; in modern civilization,
    95–97; relational issues and,
    135–137; repression and, 101

"Daydreaming," 67–68
"Dearly Beloved," 64
Dement, Iris, 123
denial, pain of, 78
dependency, 14
desire, one-way, 113
Dewey, John, 31
direct attunement, 108
discrepant awareness, 112
discussion format, 148
distress: emotion language of, 48;
    grief *v.*, 51–52
"Don't Think Twice (It's All
    Right)" (Dylan), 8, 100
drama theory, 57, 112
"Dream When You're Feeling
    Blue," 99
Durkheim, Emile, 82–83

Dylan, Bob, 8, 100
dysfunctional relationships,
119–120

EL. *See* Emotional Lability
Elias, Norbert, 82, 95
embarrassment, 40, 50, 95, 126
emotional issues, helpful lyrics
about, 143–144
Emotional Lability (EL), 12
emotional risks, 128–129
emotion language: ambiguous,
4; of anger, 49; of anxiety,
47–48; cultural differences in,
46; discussion of, 53–56; of
distress, 48; in English, 46–47;
of fear, 47–48; of grief, 48; of
love, 48; of pride, 47; problem
of, 43–45; relationships and,
56–58; of sadness, 48; of shame,
50–53; taken for granted, 44
emotions: assumptions about,
18; basic, 45; beliefs and,
10–13; cognitions *v.*, 11–12;
commercial films arousing,
12; defenses against, 44–45;
distance from, 57; domain
of, 11; facial expressions of,
46, 51; gender differences in
management of, 55; importance
of, 122–124; intolerance of,
123–124; in jealousy, 113;
love accompanied by, 5–8;
missing, 4; name chart, 55t;
need for meaning through, 124;
popular songs evoking, 1–2,
12–13; problem of naming,
9–10; questions about, 1–2;
relationships linked to, 15;

thought and, 10–13; value of,
10–13. *See also* curtailment
of feeling; emotion language;
hidden emotions
emotionworld, 28
empathetic connectedness, 37–38
empathy, equality of, 107–108
"End of the Road," 6, 77
English language: emotion words
in, 46–47; love defined by,
3–4, 24–25; modernization
influencing, 56; quality of
relationships described in,
13–14
engulfed bond, 36
engulfment, 14, 82, 105–106,
140–141
"Everybody Loves a Lover," 137,
145
"Every Breath You Take," 68
expanded view, 74–76, 80, 137

facial expressions, of emotions,
46, 51
family love, signs of, 55t
fear, 47–48, 53–54, 55t
feelings: abstract, 8; amplification
of, 125; domain of, 11; parental,
109–110. *See also* curtailment
of feeling
films, emotions aroused by, 12
fondness, 23
"A Fool in Love," 100
French folk songs, 2
Freud, Sigmund, 23, 95
Frith, Simon, 1

gender, in emotion management,
55

genuine love: applications of,
105–108; components of, 135;
connectedness and, 103–120;
defined, 104, 119; models of,
137–141; social integration and,
36
Goffman, Erving, 18, 40–41
"Goin' Out of My Head," 66
Good Will Hunting, 111
"The Great Pretender," 98
grief: distress *v.*, 51–52; emotion
language of, 48; in heartbreak
lyrics, 5–7, 9, 75, 125–126, 134;
normal, 123; pain and, 5–6;
signs, 55t; unresolved, 52
guilt, 95

Harvey, P. J., 121, 127
"Have You Ever," 70
heartbreak lyrics: alienation and,
131–135; anger in, 7–8, 125,
132, 134; chief characteristics
of, 75–76; compulsion in,
76–77; connectedness and,
135–136; constricted view in,
76; curtailment of feeling in,
7–8, 78; expanded view in,
76, 80; grief in, 5–7, 9, 75,
125–126, 134; helpful, steps
toward, 143; hidden emotions
in, 8–10; impairment in,
75–76; infatuation lyrics *v.*,
75; Korean, 91n5; language
of, 125–129; as largest love
song category, 4, 59–60; of
mourning, 76; pain in, 3,
75–76, 78, 132; patterns
in, 63–67; revenge in, 7–8;
sadness in, 134; shame and,
127, 134–135; survey of, 62,
62t
helpful lyrics, steps toward,
143–145
hidden emotions: in heartbreak
lyrics, 8–10; relationships
influenced by, 116–117; shame,
122, 124–125, 135
hospice workers, 123
hostility, 117
"How Do I Live," 87
hurt, 9
Huxley, Aldous, 19
hypercognition, 123–124

"I Am a Rock," 94, 100
idealization, 114
identity. *See* shared identity
"I Don't Know Why I Love You
Like I Do," 104
"I Get Weak," 70
"I Just Want to Be Your
Everything," 68
"I Love How You Love Me," 79,
136
"All Shook Up" (Presley), 65–66,
70
"I'm a Sixty Minute Man," 86
"I" messages, 107
impairment: in heartbreak lyrics,
75–76; in infatuation lyrics,
67–71; I–We balance and, 71;
mental, 67–71, 75–76; physical,
67, 69–71, 75–76
individual desire, in romance
lyrics, 88
individualism: pressure for, 40;
relationships and, 80–82, 84;
taken for granted, 18, 53

"I-ness," 106, 118–119
infants: caretakers' relationships
     with, 26, 81, 110; parental
     feelings toward, 109–110
infatuation: alienation and, 131–
     135; alternatives to, 141–143;
     attachment and, 115; attraction
     and, 115; attunement and, 115;
     at distance, 36–37; intuitive,
     65; love *v.*, 23–24, 48, 113–116;
     questioning authenticity of,
     144; types of, 65
"Infatuation," 69
infatuation lyrics: chief
     characteristics of, 65–67,
     71–75; constricted view in,
     74–75; heartbreak lyrics *v.*, 75;
     impairment in, 67–71; love at
     first sight, 63–65; pain in, 65;
     patterns in, 63–67; pleasure in,
     65–66; rock and roll, 84–85;
     seeing actual person, 71–74;
     survey of, 4–5, 59–60, 62, 62t;
     unrealistic, 71
integration. *See* social integration
intersubjectivity, 31–32, 81–82,
     104
intuitive infatuation, 65
Iraq War memorial, 10–11, 123
"I Saw You Standing There,"
     63–64, 73
isolation: defending against, 40;
     as form of alienation, 14, 82;
     models of genuine love and,
     140–141; between partners,
     107
"I Think I'm in Love," 66
"It Only Hurts When I'm
     Breathing," 6, 8

"I've Got to Get You into My Life,"
     85
"I've Told Every Little Star," 70,
     72–73, 133
I–We balance: impairment and,
     71; solidarity and, 82
"I Will Follow Him," 73

jealousy: emotions in, 113; as
     pseudo-love, 112–113, 116; risk
     of, 129
"Just One Look," 63

Kaufman, Gershen, 122, 127–
     128
Keys, Alicia, 133
kin, idealization and vilification
     of, 114
King Lear, 114
Korean heartbreak lyrics, 91n5

"The Lady in Red," 80, 136, 142
language, 4, 32, 125–129. *See
     also* emotion language; English
     language
"Lately," 6, 77
"Laughing on the Outside (Crying
     on the Inside)", 78, 97
Lazare, Aaron, 52–53
"Let Me Let Go," 77
"Let's Spend the Night Together,"
     86
leveling, 107
Lewis, Helen, 122
Lewis, Leona, 87, 132, 134
limbic communication, 26, 46
limerance, 25, 65
"Long Ago and Far Away," 64, 84
long-term relationships, 119

love: assumptions about, 18;
careful use of, 143; dictionary
defining, 20–21; emotional
risks of, 128–129; emotion
language of, 48; emotions
accompanying, 5–8; English
language defining, 3–4,
24–25; family, 55t; at first
sight, 63–65; infatuation *v.*,
23–24, 48, 113–116; kinds of,
108–113, 109t; lyrics defining,
1–2, 9, 17; mysterious, 2;
non-erotic, 108–110, 109t;
pain of, 3, 21, 41; pleasure of,
3, 41; practical applications
of, 117–119; pseudo-, 109,
112–113, 116; relationships
generating, 24–25; requited,
4–5, 131–135; scholarly
literature on, 23–24, 90; as
secondhand emotion, 145; as
shared identity, 24, 27–30,
35–36, 40, 104–105; solidarity
and, 30–35; subversive
investigation of, 17–18;
three components of, 26–27;
vernacular meaning of, 17,
19–20, 24. *See also* genuine
love; romantic love
Love (Stendhal), 22–23
love songs: ballads, 84–85;
delivery of, 85; importance of
emotions in, 122–124; liberties
taken by, 3; miscellaneous
category of, 5, 59, 62t;
relationship types implied in,
13–14; about requited love,
4–5; titles of, 59–60; in Top 40,
4–5. *See also* heartbreak lyrics;

infatuation lyrics; romance
lyrics
"Love Walked In," 63
loveworld, 28
loyalty, 106
lyrics: about anger, 143;
curtailment, types of, 97–101;
helpful, steps toward, 143–145;
infatuation, 59–60; love
defined by, 1–2, 9, 17; music
dominating, 85; overlapping
types of, 86–87; projects for
improving, 147–150; relational
problems with, 135–137;
sexually explicit, 5; writing
contest, 149–150. *See also*
heartbreak lyrics; infatuation
lyrics; romance lyrics

market considerations, 89
Marx, Karl, 83
mass entertainment, 124
Mead, G. H., 81
mediation, 96
"Memory" (Roethke), 144
mental impairment, 67–71, 75–76
miscellaneous category, of love
songs, 5, 59, 62t
missing emotions, 4
models of genuine love, 137–141
modernization, 56, 95–97
"Moonlight Becomes You," 73
mourning: heartbreak of, 76;
model experience of, 138
music, lyrics dominated by, 85
mutual attunement, 110–112
mutual identity. *See* shared
identity
mutual obsession, 115

mutual understanding, 32–33
"My Favorite Mistake," 77

Nagel, Thomas, 34
narcissism, 33–34
"Night and Day," 69, 84
1960s, cultural revolution of, 94
"Nobody Knows," 8–9, 78, 94,
 126, 134
non-attached idealization, 114
non-erotic affection, 111
non-erotic love, 108–110, 109t
"No One" (Keys), 133
"No One Knows," 94
"No Time to Cry" (Dement), 123

obsession, mutual, 115
obsessive non-erotic idealization,
 114
one-way desire, 113
On Love (Ortega y Gasset), 23
"On the Sunny Side of the Street,"
 98
optimal distance, 32, 57
Ortega y Gasset, José, 23
Other Minds, 81
"Over and Over," 124–125
overt proposition genre, 85–86

pain: as abstract feeling, 8; of
 denial, 78; grief and, 5–6; in
 heartbreak lyrics, 3, 75–76, 78,
 132; in infatuation lyrics, 65;
 of love, 3, 21, 41; of rejection,
 9
parental feelings, toward infants,
 109–110
patriotism, 106
pendulation, 32–33, 57–58

personality, relationships and,
 33–34
"The Phoenix and the Turtle"
 (Shakespeare), 29
physical impairment, 67, 69–71,
 75–76
Piercy, Marge, 118
pleasure: in infatuation lyrics,
 65–66; of love, 3, 41
popular songs: applicable to real
 world, 15; classes on, 147–149;
 confusing picture provided by,
 43; emotions evoked by, 1–2,
 12–13; realistic descriptions
 in, 2; scholarly literature on, 1;
 types of, 62t
power, integration and, 83–84
Presentation of Self in Everyday Life
 (Goffman), 40–41
Presley, Elvis, 65–66, 70
"Pretend," 98
Pretty Woman, 113
pride, 47, 55t
pride/shame conjecture, 40,
 116–117
projects, for improving lyrics,
 147–150
P.S., I Love You, 141–142, 144
pseudo-love, 109, 112–113, 116
psychotherapy, 96
The Purple Rose of Cairo, 114

quarrels, 107

rejection: pain of, 9; shame of, 54,
 126–127
relational issues: curtailment of
 feeling and, 135–137; helpful
 lyrics about, 144–145

relationships: balanced, 118–119; close, 129; dysfunctional, 119–120; emotion language and, 56–58; emotions linked to, 15; hidden emotions influencing, 116–117; individualism and, 80–82, 84; of infants and caretakers, 26, 81, 110; long-term, 119; love generated by, 24–25; love songs implying, 13–14; personality and, 33–34; quality of, 13–14
Remains of the Day, 111
repression, 101
requited love, 4–5, 131–135
respectful assertiveness, 107
revenge, 7–8
righteous anger, 96
rock and roll, 84–85
Roethke, Theodore, 144
role-playing, 148
romance lyrics: alienation in, 75; changes in, 84–88, 101; delivery of, 85; expanded view in, 74–75; genres of, 85; individual desire in, 88; patterns in, 63–67, 88; significant words in, 60; social integration and, 89; Spanish, 91n5; survey of, 60, 62, 62t
romantic love: attachment and, 103; attunement and, 104–105; components of, 103–106; empirical study of, 25; as pathological, 22, 25, 66–67; sexual attraction and, 26, 103, 110; signs, 55t; unrequited, 116
Rorem, Ned, 144
Rosenberg, Marshall, 37–38

sadness: attachment and, 39–40; emotion language of, 48; in heartbreak lyrics, 134
Sappho, 21–22
"(I Can't Get No) Satisfaction," 86
secondary attunement, 108
secure bond, 35–37
self-estrangement, 83
sentimentality, 73
sexism, sexuality *v.*, 144
sexual attraction: infatuation and, 115; romantic love and, 26, 103, 110; simplicity of, 27
sexuality, sexism *v.*, 144
sexually explicit lyrics, 5
sexual perversion, 34
Shakespeare, William, 29
"Shake Your Bon-Bon," 70
"Shame" (Harvey), 121, 127, 144
shame: acknowledgment of, 128, 143–144; alternative words for, 54–55; confusion about, 121–129; emotion language of, 50–53; heartbreak and, 127, 134–135; hidden, 122, 124–125, 135; meaning of, 120; modernization and, 95, 97; in pride/shame conjecture, 40, 116–117; of rejection, 54, 126–127; signs, 55t; in Top 40, 124–127
shared awareness, 107, 118–119
shared identity: communication changing, 106; love as, 24, 27–30, 35–36, 40, 104–105
Simon and Garfunkel, 94, 100
"Sittin Up in My Room," 68
social-emotional world, key dimensions of, 56–58